Gráinne Hamilton and Jen Kelchner are systems thinkers and bridgemakers who help organisations transform.

MESH

A human-centric organisational
design for a decentralised world

Gráinne Hamilton & Jen Kelchner

foreword by Bryan D. Eldridge

Copyright 2022 Interchange
All rights reserved
Printed in the United States of America

10 9 8 7 6 5 4 3 2 1

No part of this publication may be reproduced, stored in or introduced into a retrieval system, or transmitted, in any form, or by any means (electronic, mechanical, photocopying, recording or otherwise), without the prior permission of the publisher. Requests for permission should be directed to publications@interchange.world.

The moral rights of the authors have been asserted.

The content of this book is intended for information purposes only and implementation of the Mesh organisational design requires context for individual application.

Library of Congress Cataloging-in-Publication Data

Hamilton, Gráinne & Kelchner, Jen.
    Mesh: a human-centric organisational design for a decentralised world / Gráinne Hamilton & Jen Kelchner
    ISBN: 979-8-9872491-0-9 (hardback)
    ISBN: 979-8-9872491-1-6 (paperback)
    Organisational leadership, Organisational development, Organisational design, Organisational behaviour, Workplace culture, Digital transformation, Human-centric, Mesh, Decentralisation, Web3, Skills Visibility, Contribution, Systems thinking

Interchange Publication titles are available at quantity discounts when purchased in bulk for your organisation or as client gifts. For details and discount information for print, contact booksales@interchange.world.

> The past and present wilt—I have fill'd them, emptied them.
> And proceed to fill my next fold of the future...
> (I am large, I contain multitudes.)
>
> Walt Whitman[1]

---

[1] Whitman, W. (1855). *Song of Myself*, 51. *Leaves of Grass*. Walt Whitman.

Contents

Epigraph

Foreword

Concept Map

Setting Context

1. Where have we been, where are we now, where are we going?	1
2. An Organisational Design	5
3. Trapped & Untapped Value	21
4. Organisational Culture	35
5. Organisational Structure	41

The Design Concept

6. Mesh Model	49

A Method for Implementation

7. Mesh Method	69

Implementing the Design

8. Mesh Mindsets	91
9. Mesh | Core	107
10. Mesh | Operational	115
11. Mesh | Global	121

Powering Performance

12. Empowering (Re)Generative People — 129

Seeing the Unseen

13. Skills Visibility — 147

Optimising Deployment

14. Contribution Visibility — 163

Managing the Mesh

15. Primer Tools — 179

Emergence

16. Web3 Solutions — 217

17. Emergence & Expansion — 225

Acknowledgments — 231

Glossary — 233

Bibliography — 245

About the Authors — 253

Foreword

The application of emerging technologies is migrating from the fringes of early-adopters and niche vertical applications to the more mainstream category of "business essential" for organisations of all sizes and sectors around the globe. Emerging technologies are de rigueur as the primary tools in the corporate toolbox for improving business execution, implementing business model innovation, and invoking market disruption for their products and services.

There are, however, basic complications stemming from this development. Due to the rapidity of the evolution of these technologies, its development and expansion is exponentially outstripping the pace of the evolution of how organisations work; structure work and teams; and collaborate both within and between teams and individuals. This increasing gap is not only stressing organisations into FOMO (fear of missing out) and the additional perceived death knell of being deemed technological laggards, but also forcing them to redress how they operate in toto.

As a result of these complications and fears, organisations are desperately seeking directions and strategies without a map, guidebook, or lighthouse to show them the way. Without sound strategies, organisations are in the unenviable position of having more potential horsepower available to them than previously imagined via emerging technology, but woefully unprepared to harness it and embrace the efficiencies and innovations these technologies offer. In addition to a general lack of strategy, most organisation's centralised approach is in clear dissonance with the decentralised technological world ushered in by Web3 and its core technologies of blockchain and AI.

All of this begs the simple question "how do organisations navigate the landscape of a technology-driven decentralised world?"

To date, traditional work models have focused on centralisation (having a central authority or at least a central line of authority), vertically drawn hierarchies, and on-premise and geographic proximity-based workers. In total, these attributes simply are not well-suited for the increasingly remote and gig-based workforce of the 4th Industrial revolution that is unfolding in real-time.

To effectively pivot and embrace the potential and flexibility of decentralisation, organisations must address the following questions as they prepare to create a bespoke strategy uniquely suited for their needs:

What are the lessons to be learned from the open movement as the workplace moves toward and its technologies are all converging toward open thinking?

Does our organisation understand how technology itself is decentralised and what can we learn from that to apply to our teams and organisations?

What relevant skills our workforce and the available workforce at large possess? How do we know who has what skills?

How do we recognize the best internal resources to help us reach our goals? Who has the talent and where do we find them and recognize their value?

This book addresses all those questions and more, bolstered by the collective decades of work in the open community by the authors. It will provide an exhaustive framework that is understandable – and more importantly, implementable! – by practitioners at any level of technological competency, from committed lifelong luddites to self-proclaimed gearheads.

Bryan D. Eldridge M.Ed has founded, mentored, and exited multiple emerging technology companies, is an international consultant and an industry-leading educator. He has created award-winning degree programmes and certifications on emerging technology with an emphasis on Web3, blockchain and AIML.

Concept Map

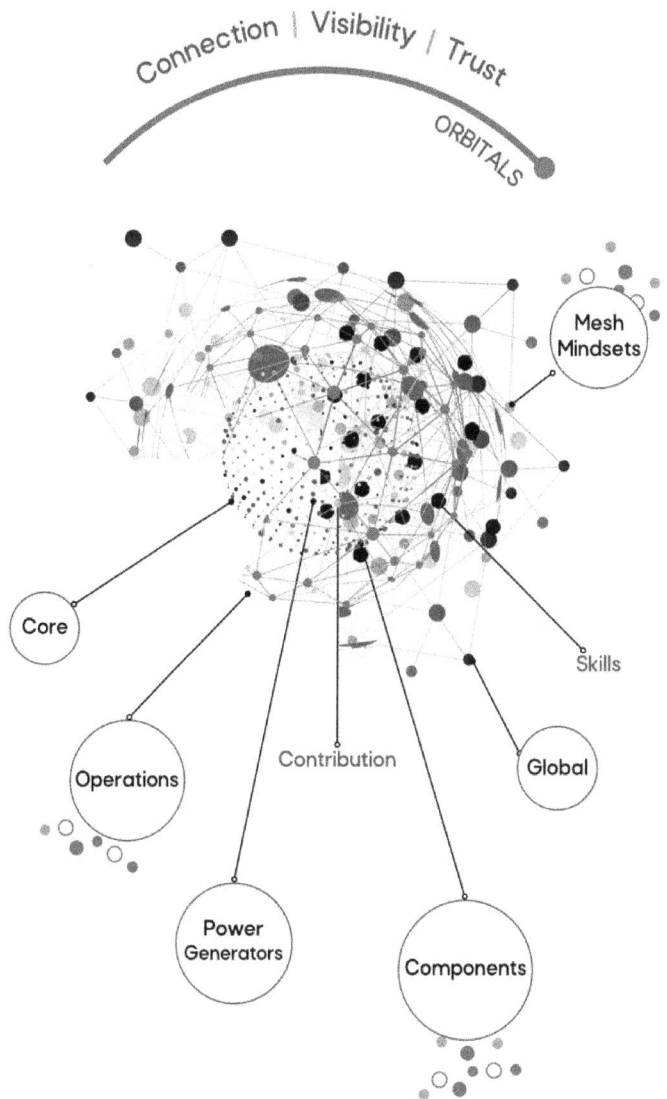

MESH CONCEPT MAP

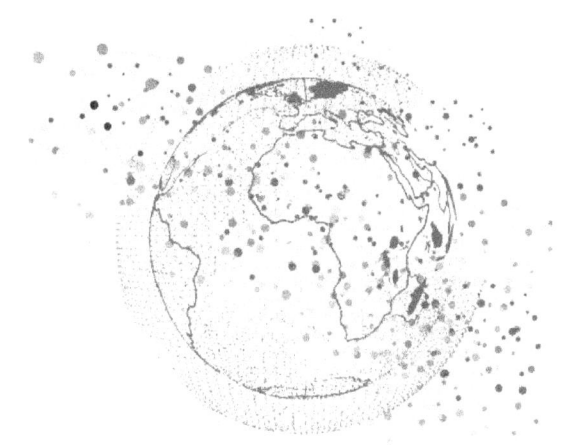

Setting Context

1.
Where have we been, where are we now, where are we going?

Revolutions: The Turning of the Wheel

Regeneration creates opportunities. The development of the wheel enabled easier travel and transportation of goods, the industrial revolution enabled mass production, and more recently the digital revolution has powered opportunities for decentralised connection across the planet. Each revolution has generated a new cycle of possibilities and requirements for powering them. How to power the current cycle, however, hasn't kept up with the pace of change. Many organisations are working with outmoded structures and processes that were appropriate for the industrial revolution but not the digitally connected world of today.

    The industrial revolution, commencing in the 18th century, saw humans move from using hand-operated tools to machines that could create more, faster. Powering those developments were organisational processes and structures that maximised consistent, repetitive effort in large buildings where machines could be housed. Preparing people to work in those contexts was formed around factory-based models that elevated being present in a certain place for a set period of time and conformance to rigid processes to deliver consistent results.[2]

We have come a long way since the industrial revolution. With the development of digital computers and the world wide web in the 20th Century, we moved into the digital revolution. A further cycle occurred with the development of hand-held devices, which concentrated the power of early computers that occupied entire rooms into something that could fit in the palm of the hand.

A significant technological and cultural revolution in the midst of this was generated by open source.[3] Diverging from the previously prevalent practice of single companies controlling proprietary products, source code for software was made openly available so that others could contribute to it. In addition, a number of other open approaches appeared, aligned by common features such as greater access and a move away from silos. Their granular forms enabled them to be reused, remixed and repurposed and they included open educational resources, open badges, open licensing and open data.[4] [5] Software, content, educational resources, skills recognition and data could now be developed and adapted

---

[2] Taylor, F. (1911) *The Principles of Scientific Management*. Harper & Brothers
[3] Peterson, C. (2018) *How I 'coined' the term open source software*. Opensource.com
[4] The Mozilla Foundation, et al. (2012) *Open Badges for Lifelong Learning*. Mozilla Foundation
[5] For more information on open approaches, please see the glossary

by distributed contributors, and rapid innovation became a hallmark of these open developments.[6]

Now, in the 21st Century, we are experiencing another revolution with the move into Web3. The developments associated with this provide the power previously generated by vast workforces concentrated around immovable machines, in a mobile and connected way.

In our increasingly decentralised world, people no longer have to travel to a particular building to work with colleagues for many jobs but can complete tasks and collaborate from geographically dispersed locations. They can use their connected devices to access decentralised data and connect that data in novel ways to provide meaningful insights and generate commercial gains, anywhere and at any time.

This presents a new set of challenges for organisations to maximise the potential of these developments, retain human connection and empower people to generate value.

---

[6] Whitehurst, J. (2015) *The Open Organization: Igniting Passion and Performance.* Harvard Business Review Press

2.
An Organisational Design

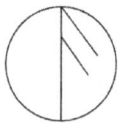

Organisational design provides a comprehensive way to improve all areas of an organisation to increase efficiency, productivity and value generation.

Organisational design provides a comprehensive way to improve all areas of an organisation to increase efficiency, productivity and value generation. By organisation we mean any group of people who organise themselves to achieve a particular purpose. This might be a business where people organise to generate income, a group of stakeholders from across a city organising to create learning pathways, or representatives from countries organising to address a global challenge.

In this book, we propose an organisational design that empowers organisations to manage the challenges and opportunities of the current and emerging context.

Three Key Challenge Areas for Organisations

Based on our work helping organisations from a range of sectors with digital transformation - including governments, political unions, private companies, education institutions, charities, cities and global communities - we have noted common areas of challenge. These can be grouped under three key areas: decentralisation, trapped & untapped value, and the emerging technology of Web3.

It is worth setting context for what we mean by these challenge areas with a brief overview of each.

Decentralisation

Decentralisation represents a move away from centralised authorities towards democratisation. It relates to decentralised technology, such as blockchains (which we will cover later in this chapter) as well as decentralised activities.

From an organisational perspective, decentralisation can be thought of as the components and the leadership, operational and engagement activities of an organisation being distributed, potentially even away from the control of the organisation. In this context, we think of decentralisation as including things like remote work, where individuals employed by an organisation connect from geographically dispersed locations rather than gathering each day in a specific set of buildings. It encompasses open contribution, such as to open source software code, where task-level rather than role-level contribution is provided by contributors who are not employed by the organisation. It also pertains to open collaboration and communities, such as where distributed stakeholders, potentially spanning multiple disciplines, sectors or countries, might coalesce around a project or idea and use common standards to connect distributed developments to achieve common aims.[7]

In terms of decentralised decision-making, this is made by a collective rather than a central authority, such as with crowdfunding, where decisions about what projects are funded, and the funds themselves, are generated through crowdsourcing platforms rather than decided upon and provided by a single venture capital group for example. Similarly, decision-making affecting a commercial company might be informed by inputs, votes or requests from an upstream community rather than by the company's leadership team alone.

---

[7] Painter, A. & Shafique, A. (2017) *Cities of Learning in the UK Prospectus*. RSA.

Components such as data may also be decentralised. Data sources that are internal and external to an organisation might be drawn on and clustered to provide useful insights. Multiple, discrete digital technology applications might also be plugged together to perform the tasks previously provided by monolithic software.

In each of these examples, the activities, decision-making and components might be distributed and controlled outside of the organisation, which presents new challenges for organisations to manage and maximise the benefits of them.

Trapped & Untapped Value

Organisations function through a mixture of processes, systems, and workflows. Over time, new processes and systems are put in place often without consideration of what came before or the potential impact to the wider ecosystem. Siloed departments, lack of information flow, and the layering of processes create pockets of trapped & untapped value (TUV). Where TUV exists, organisational growth is inhibited.

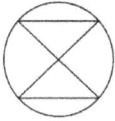

Trapped & untapped value is value that is available to an organisation but is not being used.

We define TUV in the following ways:

Trapped value is any limitation or impediment that is creating an inability to realise a goal.

Untapped value is overlooked, unseen or undervalued opportunities, connections and resources.

An easy way of identifying if TUV exists in an organisation is by following the symptoms. These include lost revenue, missed opportunities, high operational costs, unbalanced teams, hidden work, high turnover and low productivity.

The causes for trapped value vary and can have many drivers such as limited thinking, outdated or redundant processes and systems, lack of standards, or unclear expectations. Untapped value is primarily caused by a lack of visibility and awareness, such as of skills, contributions and resources that already exist and are underutilised or undervalued in the organisation and its wider ecosystem.

TUV leads to barriers in growth, expansion and innovation, and blocks the full potential value in the organisation from being released.

Web3

Web3 is the next stage of the world wide web.[8] It moves us on from the static web of limited connections and hyperlinks of Web1, past the centralised and dynamic web of ubiquitous creating, sharing and communication of Web2, to a decentralised, user-controlled web of Web3. A definition for Web3 is still evolving but broadly speaking, Web3 includes consensus-based governance, decentralisation, artificial intelligence (AI), blockchains, cryptocurrencies, user-controlled data, tokenization and smart contracts.

Web3 presents a different context for organisations. While it is not our purpose in this book to dive into the specific technological aspects of Web3, an overview is necessary for considering key features that define Web3 and their implications for how organisations organise themselves to achieve the purposes they have decided upon. As such, the following provide brief and generic introductions to Web3 elements, with an example to aid context.

---

[8] Ashmore, D. (2022) A *brief history of Web3.0*. Forbes

AI can be thought of as machine generated intelligence or learning that helps the machine to refine how it makes decisions or presents information to a user.

Example: an online store learns from the aggregated purchasing data of all users to make recommendations to a single user when they are making a purchase, to inform them about what other people who made a similar purchase also bought.

dApps are decentralised applications that operate on blockchains and can autonomously fulfill smart contracts.

Example: apps that allow users to buy and sell tokens.

Blockchains enable transactions to be managed collectively by a network, through consensus-based governance, rather than by a controlling authority. They are ledgers of facts and transactions that provide immutable records through cryptography. Information is stored in 'blocks' on nodes, which are connected across a decentralised network and facts and transactions are verified when the distributed blocks in the network (the ledger) agree. All public blockchains are open source and embed open principles through the consensus-based governance of how they are managed and extended.

Example: cryptocurrencies such as Bitcoin or Ethereum, though blockchains can be used beyond currency for other activities that benefit from transparency, security and user control.

Cryptocurrencies use blockchain technology to manage financial transactions.

Example: an individual manages currency belonging to them via a crypto wallet application on their digital device.

Smart contracts enable granular, discrete contracts to be automatically executed, controlled or verified. These can be considered trustless transactions because trust is baked in through the visibility of the exchange and the lack of the need of intermediaries to perform the tasks associated with the contracts.

Example: upon completion of a specific work task, the contributor is automatically remunerated with cryptocurrency.

Tokenization describes how assets (tokens) can be represented on a blockchain. They can take advantage of the immutability and security of the blockchain and be transferred in user-controlled ways, rather than requiring an intermediary.

Example: tokens might be used by a community to vote on how they wish philanthropic funds to be distributed.

User-controlled data is enabled by the nature of Web3. The aim is that users will have a single account controlling their data, which they can use to populate numerous applications they engage with, from their social media accounts to shopping e-commerce forms. Assets that might previously have been managed by an intermediary also now come under user control, such as assets (tokens) listed on blockchains.[9]

Example: a user maintains the deeds to their house on a blockchain rather than with a bank or legal firm.

These features of Web3 provide numerous opportunities for organisations to gain better insights, enhance connection, and to generate trust for organisational benefit while also presenting organisations with the challenge of how to integrate and maximise them.

An Organisational Design

Where does this leave us in terms of organisational design? Within the digital revolution, every organisation has become a technology organisation. It is almost impossible for an organisation to avoid the use of digital technologies in some form or another, with digital technologies having a significant impact on how organisations work, learn and connect. Within this context, many organisations use open source software or open approaches, and the teams that manage and implement them often adopt open cultural practices to aid rapid development and deployment. The cultural practices and behaviours that empower open source teams have been articulated by the global open knowledge community, the Open Organization, as the open

---

[9] Testbook. (2022) *Web 3-0*. Testbook.com

characteristics of adaptability, transparency, inclusivity, collaboration, and community.[10]

The open, transparent and decentralised nature of Web3 technologies, however, moves the need for open practices beyond the realm of technology teams and compels much wider application of decentralised and open practices in order for organisations to engage with the emerging technologies effectively and maximise their use. From a digital technology perspective, therefore, organisations are at a threshold point from which they will move on from an era where open practices were considered the purview of discrete teams, to an era where open practices will need to be adopted more widely - by organisations as a whole - in order to navigate Web3.

In order to consider open practices within the context of Web3, it is useful to examine the characteristics of what we are dealing with.

We have already introduced open approaches and the features that connect them. If we were to define the core common features of these, they might be considered to be:

- *Granularity, Flexibility, Reusability*

The cultural practices and behaviours that power open source teams have been condensed into the tenets of:

- *Transparency, Participation, Community*[11]

---

[10] The Open Organization Ambassadors. (2017) *The Open Organization Definition*. The Open Organization

[11] Whitehurst, J. (2015) *The Open Organization: Igniting Passion and Performance*. Harvard Business Review Press

Meanwhile, characteristics of Web3 tend to revolve around the following tenets:

- *Transparency, Autonomy, Decentralisation*[12]

What we can see is that these tenets converge - with transparency, and to an extent by the affordances for usage provided by granular and autonomous components, which can be reused in flexible and novel ways. They also could be considered to diverge somewhat - with participation and community versus autonomy and decentralisation. The open characteristics elevate the idea of people coming together to actively participate and co-create in community, whereas the Web3 tenets emphasise an infrastructure that enables distributed components that may or may not collaborate to develop outputs but may still connect in an organisational context. (An example of this might be distributed individuals voting within decentralised autonomous organisations (DAOs)).

So how do we bring these three views of open together - the common features of open approaches, open source cultural characteristics and Web3 - through organisational design? In order to connect them, to bridge into the new era and beyond, we think a slightly reframed set of tenets is beneficial. As such we have defined new tenets, which we think capture the convergences, and connect the

---

[12] 101 Blockchains. (2022) *The Ultimate Web3 Cheat Sheet*. 101 Blockchains

divergences, of open and Web3, whilst also expanding upon them.

The Tenets

From an organisational design perspective, we use tenets to express the values that inform an organisational culture and structure and to aid consideration of practices that help generate them. As such, they are powerful tools in an organisational design and we are intentional about how we express them.

For the purposes we have set out, we think the tenets of ***connection, visibility and trust*** help bridge between open and Web3.

Connection

The granular, flexible and reusable nature of open approaches means components can be connected and reconnected in multiple ways for different purposes. We have unified these features with the open characteristics of collaboration and community into the tenet of ***connection***. This tenet also speaks to the digital connections that are generated via Web3 tools such as blockchains, while highlighting the need to connect individuals within a decentralised context.

Visibility

We have reframed transparency with the tenet of *visibility* as we think it is suggestive of choice and speaks to an aspect of organisational design that we will explore later in the book, which is to make the unseen visible. The concept of transparency has become a cause of concern for many as it has become synonymous with the centralising forces of Web2, which undermined the idea of personal privacy in order to capitalise on people's data. We think visibility presents a more nuanced version of transparency, and we use it to represent the need to balance the benefits of transparency with privacy to generate trust, and to enable choice in what is shared. The user-control that is a feature of Web3 helps to address some of these transparency and privacy issues.

For us visibility also goes beyond the interpretation commonly applied with the open characteristics, where transparency is generally considered only in terms of making code and work open for others to see, in relation to accessibility, and the sharing of failures and successes. There is a known challenge in open contribution of free and hidden work, which affects the sustainability of open projects and open source itself.[13] While some work is underway to articulate and define the value of open source contributions,

---

[13] Pennington, H. (2019) *Open source has a working-for-free problem.* Tidelift

additional work is needed to consider how to recognise and remunerate the work of contributors and maintainers. We explore aspects of this later on in the book.

Trust

Trust is missing from the five open characteristics as articulated by the Open Organization, and is often talked about in terms of assuming positive intent, security, inclusivity, or as simply a by-product of employing the open characteristics. We think it is more than this and that it deserves to be highlighted in and of itself. We believe trust is fundamental to the notion of human-centricity within a decentralised world, and that a focus on trust practices such as personal agency and psychological safety are required for the new era of Web3. Web3 also enables secure, trustless transactions through blockchains and in the form of smart contracts, where trust is built in through the visibility of the exchange. As such trust is a key factor of Web3.

Connection, Visibility & Trust

These tenets of *connection, visibility and trust* inform an organisational design that we call **Mesh**. It is built around an open, regenerative culture and empowered by a granular, mesh structure that is primed for navigating Web3 technology. The design has been informed by our work creating, trialling and iterating improvements on legacy models, and helping organisations to bridge towards hybrid or decentralised organisational structures. It draws on lessons learned from implementing open source technology and open approaches, and through our work creating open technology and cultural standards that enable a move away from monolithic, siloed solutions, to more flexible, granular ones primed for reuse, remix and repurpose.

We think that the Mesh organisational design provides a potent way for organisations to become more human-centric, to power performance, see the unseen and optimise deployment. In this book we will examine how organisational value can become trapped or be untapped, and how organisations can use a mesh approach to release that value. We will consider how an open, regenerative culture and granular, mesh structure can optimise decentralised components and assets for flexibility and evolution and empower generative performance. Finally we will explore examples of how Web3 tools can help organisations gain insights, manage the mesh and release the fullest extent of the value available to them.

3.
Trapped & Untapped Value

Decentralisation and Web3 create unprecedented opportunities to gain rapid organisational and commercially beneficial insights, to create connections and to build trust. They also create new challenges for organisations looking to optimise and manage them.

So how can organisations release the value of these developments and maximise their benefits? To respond to this, first of all we will explore how value can become trapped, or be untapped in all types of organisations, not just those working in decentralised ways. We will consider how blocked value can impact performance, processes and overall organisational success before moving on to how this value can be released.

Burnout: Performance TUV

Increasing numbers of people are resigning from employment. This has been referred to as the Great Resignation, and studies following the Covid-19 pandemic indicate that it is being driven by burnout, which could be affecting anywhere from 43%[14] to 89%[15] of employees. Overwork and extreme mental and emotional stress are contributing to this burnout, with factors impacting negative stress including not feeling valued, not having space to learn or grow, and not feeling empowered at work.

The full value that an individual can bring to a team and organisation will be trapped if they are not enabled to contribute at their best. Dehumanising practices that treat individuals like machines, and inhibit their naturally generative processes such as curiosity, exploration, failure and iteration will diminish their ability to generate value for the organisation.

The intense innovation of the open source technology sector in the early part of the 21st century has demonstrated that the rapid development of new solutions requires curiosity and failure - exploring ideas, failing, iterating, tweaking ideas, trying again and failing again is a fundamental part of the development cycle of a robust solution.[16] This rapid innovation cycle is blocked if the opportunity to learn from failure is not an accepted part of the organisation's culture or because individuals are afraid to be judged negatively by stakeholders with whom they are collaborating. When individuals in a team do not feel psychologically safe because they feel there will be negative

---

[14] Gloat. (2021) *Great Resignation Research Report*. Gloat
[15] Visier. (2022) *Burnout Epidemic Report*. Visier
[16] Whitehurst, J. (2015) *The Open Organization: Igniting Passion and Performance*. Harvard Business Review Press

consequences if they suggest ideas which are not quite right at first, they will be inhibited from exploring ideas and potentially coming up with solutions.[17]

Value is likely to be trapped when individuals have no sense of personal agency or ownership of their work. A micromanaging boss will deplete their colleagues of agency and inhibit opportunities for value generation by them. When micromanaged, individuals tend to mirror the lack of confidence they believe the manager has in their abilities, resulting in them questioning their own ideas and initiative.[18] When an individual is not trusted or enabled to move things forward themselves or see their idea through to fruition, it denies them the satisfaction of seeing their contribution benefitting a wider context. This inhibits a sense of pride in work and of well-being not linked to remuneration. When personal agency is blocked, therefore, an easy and inexpensive opportunity to release value is missed.

Without personal agency and psychological safety, effective collaboration will be stifled. Individuals are unlikely to speak up and contribute ideas, and when their contribution is not recognised they will question why they should do anything above the bare minimum. A 'hero model' leader may pass off the ideas of others as their own to enhance perception by their bosses and aid their career

---

[17] Edmondson, A. (1999) *Psychological Safety and Learning Behavior in Work Teams*. Sage Publications
[18] Parker, S. K.. et al (2020) *Remote Managers are Having Trust Issues*. Harvard Business Review

trajectory but ultimately it will leave individuals in their teams feeling unvalued and unmotivated. This lack of motivation leads to underperforming teams and the loss of the generative power of multiple ideas and invested people.

When individuals in a team are more interested in protecting their own careers and only celebrating their individual contributions, they are more likely to compete with each other rather than work as a cohesive unit to develop solutions. This can result in individuals looking on other team members as potential rivals to the recognition they could gain to enhance their own career trajectory, which will lead to them not sharing ideas or bringing the full extent of their expertise to the collaborative effort.

Without networks and information flow, opportunities for developing deep engagement with customers, partners and external stakeholders, can also result in TUV. Personal, professional and social media networks can amplify messaging about an organisation and if the majority of individuals within an organisation share news via their networks, it can be an effective way of growing and sustaining who is brought along on the organisation's journey.

This opportunity for engagement will be curtailed if individuals do not know how to create or sustain networks, are not clear on what or if they can share, or if the organisation tries to hijack their personal networks. With a lack of clarity on the types of content that can and cannot be shared externally there is a tendency not to share anything at all rather than inadvertently share something that might be viewed negatively by the organisation. Being too specific about what individuals should share can also be damaging. Dictated messaging lacks the individual's voice, rendering it inauthentic sounding - something that will be picked up by those engaging with it. Over time this can result in a loss of trust in not only that form of organisational messaging but potentially with the organisation overall.

When it comes to the people in an organisation, when individuals do not have personal agency, do not feel psychologically safe, and are not empowered to connect, their power to generate and regenerate value for the organisation will be blocked.

Black Out: Skills TUV

When aspects of an organisation are unseen there is increased likelihood of value being trapped or untapped. Blackouts in parts of an organisation's operations will reduce insights that can be used to improve performance, processes and commercial success.

A significant contributor to TUV in organisations is a lack of skills visibility. When individuals do not feel their skills are seen or recognised, or they are unable to adequately see or articulate their skills themselves, morale and motivation is likely to be reduced.[19]

Skills cannot be deployed across an organisation to optimise the value they can bring if individuals are unaware of their skills or cannot articulate them. Research shows that many people, particularly those from disadvantaged backgrounds, can struggle to articulate their strengths and often lack awareness of, and confidence in their ability to attain a range of potentially fulfilling and rewarding career or learning opportunities.[20,21] As a result, they often fail to engage with opportunities that could ultimately lead to rewarding careers, meaning skills that organisations could potentially access remain untapped.

In organisations where there is a culture of not contributing outside of rigidly defined roles or teams, expertise that does exist within the organisation is not tapped to optimise wider organisational success. Where roles are fixed and rigid, there is often no granular insight to the skills that exist within the organisation. Skills are inextricably tied to roles rather than being seen as assets that can be drawn on across the organisation and deployed to projects and initiatives where they could be used best.

---

[19] Savitz-Romer, M & Bouffard, M. (2012) *Ready, Willing and Able. A Developmental Approach to College Access and Success*. Harvard Education Press

[20] Markus, H & Nurius, P. (1986) *Possible Selves*. American Psychologist 41(9):954-969

[21] Freeman, K. (2004) *African Americans and College Choice. The Influence of Family and School*. SUNY Press

Limited or no tools to enable visibility of granular skills, means they cannot be discovered or deployed across an organisation optimally.

A lack of skills visibility can also impact retention. When individuals can see opportunities to grow and pathways stemming from skills inherent to their interests, retention is increased because when work is linked to intrinsic motivation (doing something because it is enjoyed) individuals are more likely to stay the course, invest in their job and overcome challenges.[22][23] Without opportunities to develop skills, to increase awareness of intrinsic motivators, or to contribute at their best, individuals are more likely to become demotivated and look around for opportunities with other organisations.

Additionally, understanding skills gaps and future skills needs is vital to organisational sustainability. When insights and the ability to proactively manage these areas are blocked, sub-optimal and disrupted organisational performance is more likely. Partnerships with the extended community surrounding an organisation through skills networks can be helpful for illuminating skills that the organisation could tap into. This might include help with identifying human capability skills that are often hidden or

---

[22] Deci, E & Ryan, R. (2010) *Intrinsic Motivation*. The Corsini Encyclopedia of Psychology

[23] Deci, E & Ryan, R. (2000) *Intrinsic and Extrinsic Motivations: Classic Definitions and New Directions.* Contemporary Educational Psychology 25,54–67 (2000)

not formally recognised, such as curiosity or empathy that may be evidenced through informal learning and recognition contexts such as volunteering.[24] Failure to tap into skills networks beyond the organisation, therefore, can limit the type of skills that can be accessed and diminish the value of skills conduits.

Lack of visibility, of skills and other unseen aspects affecting organisations, can block opportunities for optimising recruitment, retention and deployment, and negatively impact overall organisational success.

Circuit Breakers: Deployment TUV

Mistrust and disempowering organisational processes can lead to malfunction of organisational circuits and a reduction in value generation.

Before the Covid-19 pandemic, organisations faced challenges created by the digital revolution, such as how to navigate the disruption caused by digital transformation, and how to keep up with the speed of innovation and remain relevant. Post-pandemic, new challenges added to the existing ones, including how to manage remote work and navigate broader societal and economic shifts.[25] These

---

[24] Hamilton, G. (2016) *Discussion Paper on Open Badges in Territories*. Open Badge Network, Erasmus+

[25] Gigauri, I. (2021) *New Economic Concepts Shaping Business Models In Post-Pandemic Era*. International Journal of Innovative Technologies in Economy, (1(33)

changes drove some organisations to make hasty decisions to restructure and reorganise in ways that were not always optimal for the new and emerging situations they found themselves in.

The pandemic led to a significant increase in remote work and decentralised teams. Within this context, some organisational leaders struggled to trust their employees without seeing firsthand that activity was taking place.[26] Media coverage of some of the more extreme examples of leaders' lack of trust, showed ubiquitous tracking that might manifest as employees being viewed on video at all times.[27] Studies found that employees resented what they saw as an invasion of privacy and a lack of trust that they were completing their work. An organisational culture that focuses on tracking and presentee-ism rather than on individuals having the flexibility to manage their workload and complete it within a given timeframe, denies personal agency, which we have already identified as a factor in inhibiting individuals from generating value.

A facet of individual contribution that organisations often choose to ignore, is hidden work. As well as work completed beyond contractual hours, this corrosive element can encompass unseen and unrecognised contribution, and undervalued and uncompensated work. In our experience,

---

[26] Parker, S. K.. et al (2020) *Remote Managers are Having Trust Issues.* Harvard Business Review

[27] Blanding, M. (2022) *Want hybrid work to succeed? Trust, don't track employees.* Harvard Business School

hidden work dehumanises individuals, can contribute to burnout, and undermines the contribution ecosystem with an unbalanced value system. This lack of insight in one part of the contribution ecosystem is compounded by a lack of awareness in another part. When an individual's preferences or tendencies for contribution, their skills and their intrinsic motivations are unknown, individuals are not enabled to contribute at their best.

Remote work and decentralisation of organisational components is likely to continue. They provide many benefits for generating organisational value and may decrease some costs, such as no longer needing to house employees in costly workplace buildings (though it is unclear yet how costs will be rearranged in terms of the home-based expenses and digital infrastructure required for hosting a remote workforce). Research shows that many individuals value the flexibility that remote work provides and are often more productive.[28] This suggests that if organisations do not focus on solutions for enabling and recognising remote contributions in a way that is trusted by employees, they risk losing valuable performance gains.

Effective contribution can be blocked through mistrust and counterproductive ways of connecting and generating awareness. This prevents individuals and teams from contributing at their best and inhibits the optimal

---

[28] Farrer, L. (2020) 5 *Proven Benefits Of Remote Work For Companies*. Forbes

deployment of contributions into services or products to generate value for the organisation.

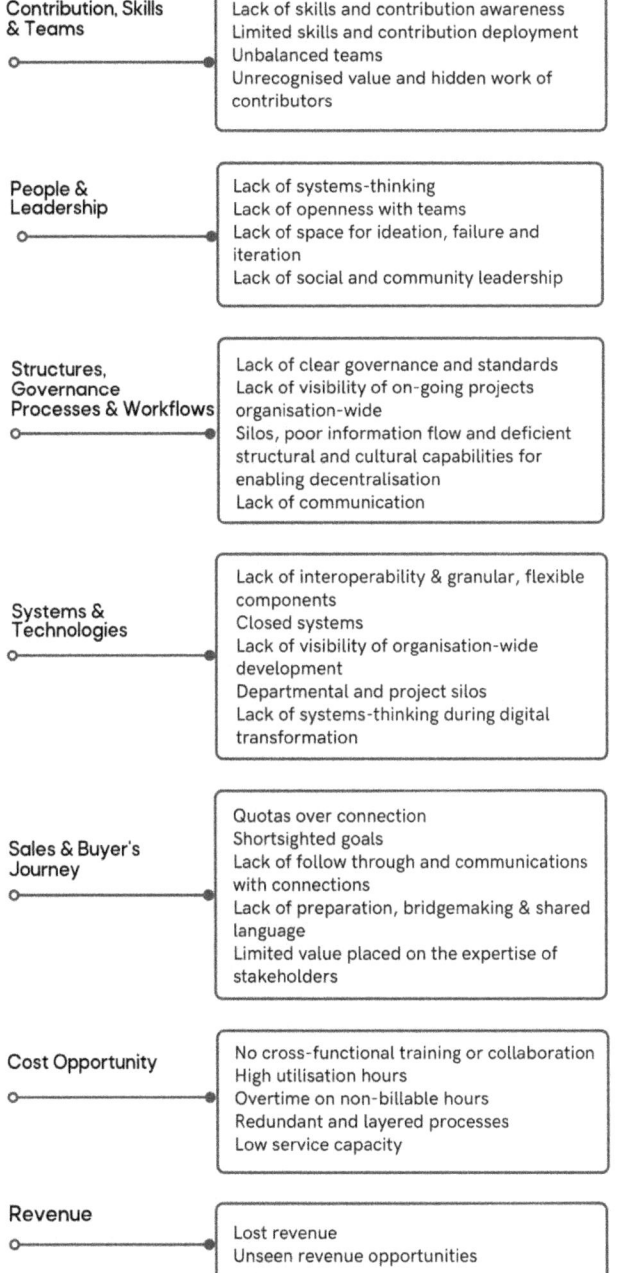

Common Examples of TUV

TUV indicators

To summarise, from an individual's perspective, certain scenarios indicate a higher likelihood of TUV being present. TUV is likely to exist where there is:

1. Lack of personal agency
2. Lack of psychological safety
3. Lack of recognition of contribution
4. Lack of positive messaging about the organisation
5. Lack of networks
6. Lack of intrinsic motivation
7. Lack of contribution outside of role
8. Lack of sharing ideas
9. Lack of idea exploration
10. Lack of feeling valued
11. Lack of learning
12. Lack of inclusion
13. Lack of ownership
14. Lack of loyalty to the organisation

Releasing TUV

The challenges brought about by TUV and decentralised ways of working, are significant. We have considered some of the ways value can become trapped or be untapped in organisations and how these can ultimately impact operational effectiveness, which inevitably leads to a loss of value generation and sustainability.

Releasing that organisational value requires changes. Small changes can add up to big shifts but for changes to be efficient and effective it is important to understand the root cause of the blocks. They may be a cultural issue, a leadership issue, a technology issue, a workflow issue, or a mixture of them all. Deeper and more nuanced organisational insights mean more precise changes can be made, yielding significant results with less disruption.

To explore how organisational cultures and structures can affect value generation and the ability to adapt, we will consider these two aspects of an organisation next.

4.
Organisational Culture

The Importance of Organisational Culture

How do leaders create vibrant and purposeful organisations and bring people along with them?

Over the past couple of decades digital technologies and open approaches have been employed by organisations to revolutionise how they work, learn and collaborate. Emerging technologies, and developments such as AI and the use of bots, have compelled consideration of how people will contribute in future and how we can collectively take a more human approach to organising for work.

While some organisations have worked to modernise their structures and design, there is still overlap of outdated processes, policies and behaviours. Since the late 1800's most organisations have followed Taylorian Models or early management theory, built around humans performing rote tasks, many of which can now be completed by technology.[29]

---

[29] Flynn, J. (1998) *Taylor to TQM: 100 years of production management.* IIE Solutions, October 1998, 22+. Gale Academic

However, in many ways, organisations haven't shifted how they work or empower people to lead.

What is Organisational Culture?

Culture is a broad term and can mean different things to different people. Some organisations might think of it as a core set of values and practices, while others will view it as their style or environment.

We have developed our ideas on organisational culture through our experiences helping organisations navigate digital transformation, through our work implementing open approaches, and by helping organisations develop and use emerging technology. These experiences have informed our understanding of the conditions that helped organisations to achieve positive outcomes and our approach incorporates lessons from each of these areas.

We will use our definition of culture as a basis for discussing it throughout the book.

Our Approach to Organisational Culture

We think of organisational culture as the values and behaviours that contribute to the unique social and psychological environment of an organisation. For us it is the ethos, values, and frameworks for how a company conducts itself internally and externally. In other words, an organisation's culture includes its core values, its expectations for behaviour, its decision-making frameworks, how information flows through the organisation and how it conducts itself with others.

Consideration of culture is crucial for organisational success as it affects contribution, performance, employee engagement, and customer relations.[30]

Through our work, we have noted in particular how the ethos and values of openness and a willingness to regenerate can help individuals organise, connect, share, collaborate and reorganise to generate significant value and resilient and sustainable outputs.

---

[30] Westrum R. (2004) A typology of organisational cultures. Qual Saf Health Care. Suppl 2:ii22-7

How Is Value Blocked Through Organisational Culture?

Insights gathered in the course of our work have shown factors that block openness and barriers organisations can face when adopting new technologies. These barriers create pockets of TUV across organisations, amongst people and leadership and in systems, structures and governance.

Conversational analysis of our work with government and public sector leaders between 2019 and 2021[31] revealed that from an open perspective, open is perceived as a continuum and requires context. Our research showed that the language and understanding of open was limited and often skewed only to open source technology development. Perception and perspectives were limited due to lack of awareness that open can be seen as a cultural approach beyond how to manage open source technology. We also found that people and leadership behaviours were considered to have a significant impact on openness and the ability to regenerate to incorporate more open ways of working.

---

[31] Hamilton, G. & Kelchner, J. (2021) *Insights Report: At the Interchange of Open Culture & Navigating Futures*. Interchange

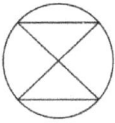

"There are challenges with implementing an open culture if we continue to only have a technology focus without cultural consciousness - it will slow organisations down"

Public sector leader, European Commission[32]

When asked about what blocked an open culture and the ability to regenerate their organisations, leaders from government and the public sector consistently identified the following challenge areas:

- Lack of psychological safety in the workplace
- Behaviours preventing connection, collaboration & adaptability among people and leadership
- Cultural conditions and mindsets that inhibited systems thinking about the impact of individual decisions on the whole organisation

---

[32] Hamilton, G. & Kelchner, J. (2021) *Workplace of the Future. Interchange masterclass*. Interchange

When asked about the barriers to implementing open source technology specifically, two factors were identified:

- Cultural structures and governance
- Dependency on open contributors, lack of available skillsets in the organisation, and lack of retention of qualified contributors

Overall, our research highlighted that behaviours, mindsets and cultural conditions can result in TUV. Furthermore, the structures and processes of an organisation can have a significant impact on enabling openness and the ease and speed of regeneration.

5.
Organisational Structure

The Frameworks of an Organisation

Architecting the structure of an organisation is much like architecting a physical structure or software solution. An end product is built, which needs foundations, individual components, conduits for information flow, and so on.

The Impact of Organisational Structures

Governance, processes, systems, workflows and how they align or can be realigned for business goals have to be considered when defining an organisational design. We will consider these elements under the heading of organisational structures.

Organisational structures influence how organisations behave through the coordination of tasks, decision-making and how information flows to help them meet their goals. Innovation and new technologies affect the individuals within an organisation, particularly when substantial, monolithic software implementations with widespread usage across the organisation are substituted for something similar. In our experience, an often overlooked area of digital transformation is the significant impact on people and leadership and the downtime that can result as individuals navigate the new processes and workflows that large-scale software changes demand.

Organisational Types

While every organisation will contain certain structural elements - governance, processes, workflows, etc - how these are applied within different organisational types can impact how they function.

Under our broad definition of an organisation - any group of people who organise themselves to achieve a particular purpose - we might further group organisations under the following categories of current organisational type: traditional, hybrid and decentralised. Each of these organisational types have certain characteristics although it is unlikely that any organisation will align strictly with any one of these and may include aspects of them all.

Traditional Organisations

Traditional organisations might be thought of as operating with fixed, hierarchical structures and may be heavily siloed. There are likely to be rigidly defined power structures in place with information typically moving from the top down. Examples of this kind of organisation might include: those with command and control structures; heavily regulated organisations; or organisations where all work is conducted in a given place at a given time.

Hybrid Organisation

A more fluid organisational type might be thought of as hybrid. Possibly more complex, this type of organisation enables more flexibility for meeting objectives within the business structure itself. A hierarchical structure may be in place yet allow for more cross-collaborative teamwork, decentralised activities or Web3 technologies. Examples of hybrid organisation types include: those that have a mix of office-based and remote working; or a traditional organisation that invites open collaboration to open source technology or regularly employs open rather than traditional approaches for software, data, or learning.

Decentralised Organisations

Decentralised organisations can be thought of as having the least centralised control of endeavours and outputs. They are likely to be connected, fluid, interoperable, collaborative and highly adaptable, and allow for swift evolution and response with information flow across all channels, engagement opportunities for individual contributors, as well as decentralised teams and communities. Examples of decentralised organisation types include: Decentralised Autonomous Organisations (DAOs) built around smart contracts and tokenization; knowledge communities; communities of practice; or organisations that form around multi-stakeholder, decentralised collaboration.[33]

How Is Value Blocked in Organisational Structures?

Insights gathered from our work suggests that when an operational lens is applied, systems, governance, and outdated structures have a significant impact on blocking or releasing value.[34] We have found that organisational value is often trapped by having limiting processes that block access to the right team members or skillsets and prevent the ability to adapt quickly. Such processes and structures for operations create blocks for open engagement and the ability to make continual small changes to enable regeneration. Insights gathered through conversational analysis of our work with government and public sector

---

[33] Sims, A. (2019), *Blockchain and Decentralised Autonomous Organisations (DAOs): The Evolution of Companies?* 28 New Zealand Universities Law Review 423-458

[34] Hamilton, G. & Kelchner, J. (2021) *Insights Report: At the Interchange of Open Culture & Navigating Futures.* Interchange

leaders, revealed that the following areas were commonly identified as presenting challenges:

- Outdated policy and governance
- Rigid working structures and processes
- Monolithic current systems and lack of interoperability

These findings relating to organisational culture and structure correlate with insights gathered through our work with other organisations - that for organisations to release optimal value, we think they need open, human-centric cultures and structures that are flexible, interoperable and able to rapidly evolve.

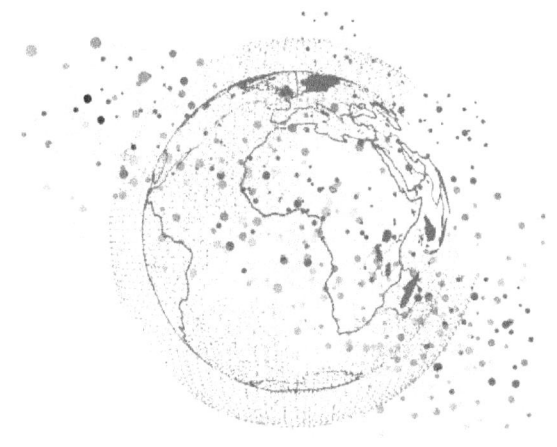

The Design Concept

48

6.
Mesh Model

Organisational Design

As we have explored, organisations exist within an increasingly decentralised context. Many people now work remotely and no longer connect in-person in an office on a daily basis. The in-person 'glue' that used to connect individuals within an organisation, through meetings and chats over coffee where informal connections might turn into support for a project or pointers to helpful resources, may no longer exist. These changes in working practices require updates to organisational design, to enable individuals - the most generative components of an organisation - to connect, communicate and mesh.

We have also explored how organisational culture and structures can create TUV, and we will assume that organisations are interested in remaining relevant and maximising the opportunities of emerging technology. Given this, we can say that an effective organisational design for current and emerging contexts, will need to help organisations manage the challenges of decentralisation, reveal and release value, and optimise for Web3 technologies.

In summary, an effective organisational design will enable organisations to:

1. Optimise for current digital technologies and decentralisation
2. Reveal and release TUV
3. Prime for and navigate Web3

To meet these requirements, we have also identified that we want to enable the tenets of connection, visibility and trust, and ideally, easy regeneration.

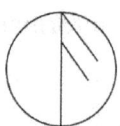

Mesh is an organisational design that helps organisations to generate connection, visibility and trust, and to regenerate.

Conceptualising the Organisational Design

To understand the processes by which these requirements might be integrated to create an open culture and a flexible structure, it is helpful to gain an overview of an organisation as a whole - to consider the entire system and how the different components of it interact. As such, in this chapter we develop a visual blueprint and draw on metaphors to illustrate the key features and principles of the design. Adopting a systems thinking approach aids understanding of the full organisational ecosystem and the identification of multiple vantage points from which to consider the functioning of the organisation.

We will start creating the model by considering the features of meshes and how a mesh structure - a network of nodes - aids flexibility and releases value.

Meshes

Many kinds of meshes can be found in nature and areas of human activity. They are networks, formed of connections that enable information to flow through nodes to the entire structure. They can be expanded with new connections and nodes. The flexible, connected structure and information flow provides opportunities for revealing and releasing value.

Releasing Value with Meshes

In spiders' webs, a mesh structure enables a spider to catch the valuable resource of food. The mesh enables information to be sent through the web to pinpoint where something has landed, directing the spider to the precise spot. *The mesh enables a spider to catch what is valuable to it.*

When Suzanne Simard discovered that trees could 'talk' to each other, it was through her research on a mesh-like mycelium layer - a network of fungus connecting tree roots.[35] Simard discovered that through this mesh, information was being sent back and forth between various trees in a stand. This information might include warnings of pests or disease impacting one tree, thereby enabling the rest of the connected trees to develop defences to fend off similar attacks. *The mesh enables trees to communicate valuable information.*

The inventor of the World Wide Web, Tim Berners-Lee, envisaged the web as empowering the flow of information through connections. In the World Wide Web, distributed content, knowledge and individuals are connected via an interwoven mesh of hyperlinks and interoperable technology. Berners-Lee has commented that these connections mirror the way neurons connect in the human brain and that it is these connections that enable

---

[35] Simard, S. (2021) *Finding the Mother Tree: Discovering the Wisdom of the Forest.* Allen Lane

humans to develop knowledge.[36] *The mesh enables people to tap into valuable information and connections.*

Factors that influence our experience of the world but are invisible or harder to see with the naked eye, were illuminated through the work of pioneering mathematician and physicist, James Clerk Maxwell. Maxwell, considered by many as the founder of electrical engineering, catalysed understanding of electromagnetism and electricity.[37] This gave rise to the mesh current method, which can be used to identify how currents flow in an electrical circuit.[38] *The mesh provides a way of describing how electricity currents flow in a circuit, to generate valuable power.*

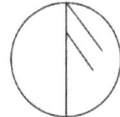

"One scientific epoch ended and another began with James Clerk Maxwell"
Albert Einstein[39]

In each of these examples, the mesh structure helps to conduct and release value.

---

[36] Berners-Lee, T. (1999) *Weaving the Web: The Original Design and Ultimate Destiny of the World Wide Web by Its Inventor.* HarperOne
[37] Maxwell, J.C. (1865) A dynamical theory of the electromagnetic field. Philosophical Transactions of the Royal Society of London. 155: 459–512
[38] Sarkar, T.K., Salazar-Palma, M., & Sengupta, D. (2010). JAMES CLERK MAXWELL: The Founder of Electrical Engineering. Syracuse University
[39] Harman, P. H. (2002) *The Scientific Letters and Papers of James Clerk Maxwell. Vol. III (1874-1879)* Cambridge University Press

Mesh Technology

Recent developments in technology also leverage the principles of meshes, connection, and flow. Mesh infrastructures exist in a few contexts and are becoming increasingly popular as a move away from monolithic, cumbersome and inflexible software to distributed, plug & play-type systems, where granular, interoperable components can be plugged together and interact.

An example of a mesh network is Wifi systems that create optimised wifi coverage in a given area by enabling a number of distributed wifi points to connect and communicate with each other to dynamically route data efficiently over as wide an area as possible.

Data mesh architecture draws on and enables management of distributed data from multiple sources rather than from a restricted set of data available within a monolithic database.[40] In this context, data usage and the insights that can be gained from ever-evolving data sources become exponentially greater. New components and data sources can be docked and added at any time due to the flexible and scalable mesh structure.

Service meshes have advanced to solve security and visibility challenges presented by distributed technology, to connect them in a trusted way. A service mesh provides a

---

[40] Dehghani, Z. (2022) *Data Mesh*. O'Reilly Media, Inc.

means to create secure communications between applications across untrusted networks, to identify other distributed components at a granular level and gain visibility to resolve issues such as load balancing for optimal delivery to the user.[41]

From a structural perspective, being able to tap into multiple connected, flexible and scalable distributed components presents extensive opportunities for powering performance, gaining insights and releasing TUV in an organisation.

So how can we enable this through an organisational design that empowers a culture and individual behaviours to optimise the opportunities of such a structure?

---

[41] Calcote, L. et al (2023) *Service Mesh Patterns*. O'Reilly Media, Inc.

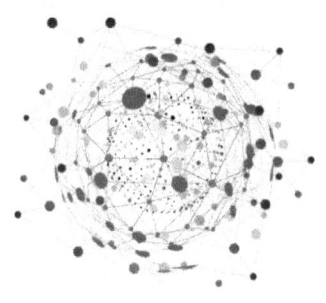

Conceptual Features

Meshes

The features of a mesh illustrate the importance of information flow to release value. Information flow is vital to the functioning of an open and partially or fully decentralised organisation. It must exist to connect the various distributed components and enable them to function effectively, to generate and regenerate as new data is passed between them.

Nodes

Adding to this concept, we can think of nodes as components that can be added to the mesh, connected to the rest of the mesh structure, and through which information can flow. These nodes are organisational components such as individuals, teams and technology through which information, such as ideas, data, and inspiration can flow. Such a structure provides opportunities for flexibility because nodes can be added, moved and connected to other nodes to provide a flexible mesh organisation that is able to adapt and evolve.

Orbs

Expanding on the features of a mesh with another useful design to be found in nature, we can extend the concept of the mesh with the benefits to be gained from orbs. An example of an orb that perhaps comes most readily to mind is a planet. The orb shape allows rapid connection and information flow across and to every part of the structure, and expanding on the planetary analogy, they can be held together by a gravitational pull and orbit other orbs.

Clusters

Clusters are a feature in all of these conceptual elements. Planets cluster together in solar systems, moons cluster and orbit around planets, and a mesh can be considered a cluster of nodes in a network. Clusters can be broken apart and re-clustered and like fractals, clusters can exist within clusters.

In clusters, patterns can be found. When different data sources are clustered they reveal new insights. When granular skills are clustered, they can illuminate previously unrecognised or unarticulated abilities. When individuals form teams, understanding the contribution tendencies of the individuals aids optimal clustering to create balanced teams.

The idea of power generation is a relevant consideration for an organisational design. The design needs to power and empower value generation for the organisation.

Power Generation

The structural elements that enable connection, information flow and clustering, empower the generation of value throughout the organisational system. Therefore, we will add to our conceptual model by considering how value is empowered and generated by the organisational design (drawing inspiration from the work of James Clerk Maxwell again). While the use of power metaphors for describing organisational processes is nothing new, we use them in a particular way, so will set out the context for how we use them below.

Within an organisation many sources power value generation, including an individual, teams, the organisational culture, technology, workflows, and the wider ecosystem. We might think of power and value generation in the following ways.

Power generation can be thought of as how individuals and other organisational components are empowered, how things get done, and how information flows.

Value generation can be thought of as the value that is generated by the contributions of individuals, teams, technologies and other organisational components.

Power Generators

The generation of power and value requires a source and receivers to amplify, conduct and distribute the power, which are informed by capabilities and capacity.

Capability

Capability may be defined as the power or ability to do something, which we might think of in terms of an individual's awareness, knowledge, beliefs, mindsets and skills. Every individual holds capabilities and each organisation holds a collective of capabilities at their disposal for powering contribution to achieve its goals.

Low capability levels are often an indicator of untapped value in contributors' skills and mindsets.

Capacity

Capacity can be defined as the amount something can contain or produce, and for our purposes we will think of it as competence. The capacity of individuals and other organisational components to take action, conduct and amplify value is dependent upon culture and structure.

Low capacity levels are often an indicator of trapped value in culture, processes, systems, technology and governance.

Power Source

At the core of the organisation, we conceptualise a power source. These are contributors, such as the leadership team, that empower the operations. Individuals can also be thought of as having an internal power source, which drives their own capacities and capabilities.

The individual's capacity to contribute is affected by their mindsets, awareness, learning agility, skills and contribution tendencies, while their capabilities for contributing will be affected by personal agency, psychological safety and how they respond to change and flexible processes.

Power Plant

The operations and processes of an organisation we can think of as a power plant. The power plant provides capacity for information to flow through and generate value, ideally with minimal resistance. Drawing on power sources, the power plant acts as a generator, container and conductor for collective contributions, balancing, optimising and sustaining them.

The power plant's capacity to meet the needs of organisational (re)generation is informed by being aware of, balancing and optimising the available capabilities.

Power Broker

We can think of the global context for an organisation as a power broker that affects the distribution, impact and influence of the collected value generated by the organisation.

The capability of the power broker to assign value to the organisation is influenced by its perception of the organisation, and this influences its capacity to share and amplify the value generated by the organisation. The power broker acts as a conduit for the organisation's collective contributions, as a resistor or amplifier, determining diminishing returns or expansion and growth.

Principles

Metaphors associated with power generation and the other conceptual features of meshes, nodes, orbs, and clusters, highlight principles that inform the Mesh organisational design. Articulating these principles aids consideration of the types of organisational behaviours and structures that help generate flexibility, trust, insights and connection.

The conceptual elements help describe a structure that can cater for granular and distributed components connected in a network, and illustrate the types of interactions and behaviours that can be supported.

For example, 'current' is sometimes used to describe connections and information flow between people, such as how a particular feeling is transmitted through a group: 'a current of excitement flowed through the team'. The word 'resistor', which describes what prevents or controls electricity currents flowing around a circuit, can be employed to consider what prevents or controls information flow around an organisation. 'Magnetic' might be used to describe a culture that draws others into its orbit, and the word mesh used to describe how people connect, as in 'they really meshed'.

Language can be an important tool for aiding implementation of sustainable organisational change and be used to inform guiding principles for making changes to organisational cultures and structures.[42]

---

[42] Nicol, D. & Draper, S. (2009) *A blueprint for transformational organisational change in higher education: reap as a case study*. The Higher Education Academy

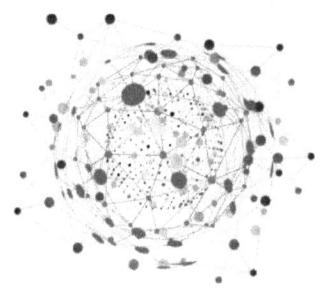

A Conceptual Model

Drawing on the principles of meshes, nodes, orbs, clusters and power generation to aid systems thinking and create a conceptual model for the design, we have:

- A central orb at the core - the power source
- An operational mesh that wraps around it so that every point is connected to others - the power plant
- A global ecosystem orbiting the organisation - the power broker

This model enables information to flow around the organisational structure, between and through nodes in the most efficient way possible and exacts a gravitational pull to draw others into its orbit.

When applied in an organisational context, the principles and features of the model manifest as, and benefit from:

- An open, regenerative culture and leadership to catalyse the components and connections in the mesh, to get the most value out of every part of the organisation, draw others into its orbit, and promote behaviours that optimise the benefits of decentralisation.

- A mesh structure to enable information flow and to capitalise on the value that can be derived from connected, granular and flexible internal and external components, such as evolving data sets and the intellectual capital of cross-organisational and external communities.
- Web3 technologies such as blockchain, tokenization, and smart contracts to improve operational processes and manage the mesh, such as AI driven visualisation tools that enable collecting, connecting and clustering of data from a variety of sources to provide helpful insights, to optimise processes, and to release value.

We will reference these elements and the principles of the model as we consider how to implement the design within an organisation.

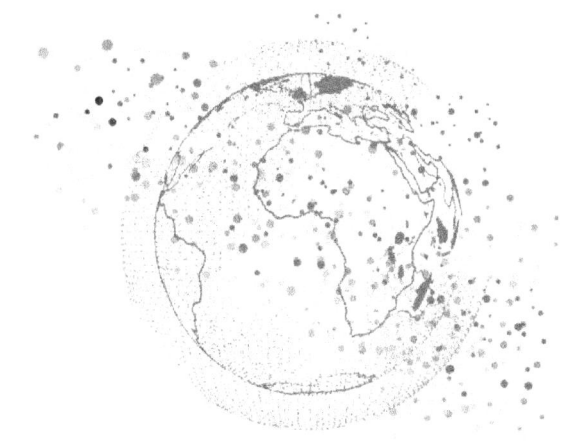

A Method for Implementation

7.
Mesh Method

Mesh Method

To help implement the principles of the Mesh design through the creation of an open, regenerative culture; a flexible, granular structure; and an environment primed for Web3 technologies, we use what we refer to as the Mesh method. This method:

- Employs the **lenses** of COG: Core, Operational and Global
- Embeds the **tenets** of: Connection, Visibility and Trust
- Applies the **conditions** of ORBITALS: Open; Regeneration; Balance; Information flow; Trust practices; Awareness; Learning; and Sustainability

Lenses aid a systems thinking approach, to gain a rounded perspective of the organisation and different vantage points for considering implementation of the Mesh design.

The **tenets** express the values that inform the organisational culture and structure, and aid consideration of practices to generate them. They are interdependent and inform each other.

Conditions catalyze the culture and aid implementation of the structure.

Lenses
COG

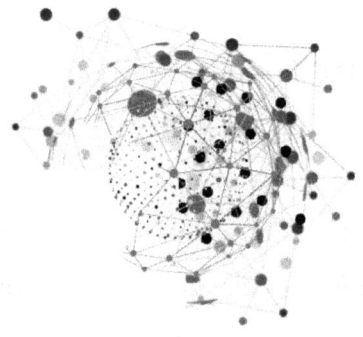

Applying different lenses offers the chance to consider different perspectives of an organisation and organisational design. The lenses of COG: Core; Operational; and Global; aid consideration of these different perspectives.

 **Core:** The leadership team; also an individual's self-awareness, and conscious and unconscious behaviours. (Orb) The *power source*.

 **Operational:** Organisational processes and frameworks. (Mesh) The *power plant*.

 **Global:** Wider context and engagement. (Orbiting ecosystem) The *power broker*.

Tenets
Connection, Visibility & Trust

The three tenets of connection, visibility and trust express the values that inform the culture and structure of mesh organisations. We will explore why they are significant here before going into more detail about how they can be operationalised in the following chapters.

Connection

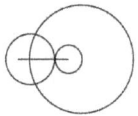

"When we try to pick out anything by itself, we find it hitched to everything else in the Universe"
John Muir[43]

The work of naturalist John Muir demonstrated how natural systems are interconnected and that the actions of one part of an ecosystem impact other parts.

Why connection is important

Solutions can be developed faster when there is connection as more ideas, insights and expertise are brought to developing a solution. Information flowing through connected components builds the collective knowledge of an organisation, be that a company, a community or a Decentralised Autonomous Organisation. Connections with customers, external stakeholders and wider communities

---

[43] Muir, J. (1911) *My First Summer in the Sierra*. Houghton Mifflin Company

also provide visibility to the organisation, enabling people to join the organisational journey and develop buy-in and trust.

If a component works in a silo, a circuit of the operational mesh is broken and the organisation cannot produce the same generative results. Therefore, to avoid silos and to promote information flow, the organisational design needs a culture and structure that promotes connection.

Enabling connection

A culture that promotes connection and information flow is formed of individuals that are willing to share, reciprocate and recognise that as part of an interdependent ecosystem, they are dependent on each other to create the best outcomes.

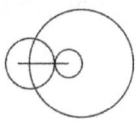

> "Governments, organisations and people working openly have demonstrated how openness can help us organise ourselves, connect, share and collaborate to build sustainable solutions."
> Hamilton & Kelchner[44]

Structures for information flow are necessary to enable connection and for collaboration and communities to form, flex, morph and re-form around different subjects or to develop solutions.

A networked approach enables the organisation to tap into value across and beyond the organisation, connecting a wide pool of expertise and perspectives. Distributed components can connect and work together effectively when processes for interoperability, discovery and connection are in place.

The use of a common set of standards will provide guiding principles for developments to align to and empower interoperability, appropriate levels of consistency and discovery. Distributed developments can be connected

---

[44] Hamilton, G. & Kelchner, J. (2021) *Insights Report: At the Interchange of Open Culture & Navigating Futures.* Interchange

through agreed behaviours and structural processes, to increase visibility, aid signposting, enable the creation of personalised pathways, and provide a network of support.[45]

Communities provide a cultural and structural role in developing connection. They provide access to many perspectives and have been demonstrated to aid the development of better and more robust products and services.[46] Communities can connect organisations to the kind of people they are trying to reach, and can raise and help them cater for eventualities a small project team might not think of alone. Such community relationships are built on trust, and drawing on the resources of communities must be reciprocated if they are to be sustainable and create a regenerative cycle of benefit.

Connection is a core tenet of mesh organisations. It aids in knowledge sharing between and across the organisation, and beyond to external stakeholders and communities. It aids sustainable regeneration and evolution by bringing together many perspectives, skills and an ecosystem of support.

---

[45] Painter, A. & Shafique, A. (2017) *Cities of Learning in the UK Prospectus*. RSA.
[46] Whitehurst, J. (2015) *The Open Organization: Igniting Passion and Performance*. Harvard Business Review Press

Connection builds information flow and trust and also needs these to function well. When these are in place, it:

- Helps generate flexibility through the timely exchange of ideas, and better outputs through access to a wide range of perspectives, experiences and skills.
- Aids in gathering insights and knowledge sharing between and across the organisation, generating a sense of ownership and resilience through connectedness.
- Promotes awareness and alignment of values, brings decentralised components together, and prompts engagement from a wide range of demographics, helping them feel part of the journey and invested in supporting the sustainability of the organisation.

Visibility

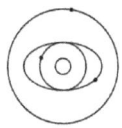

"Web3, for me, is not cryptocurrency, it's not blockchain, it's not tokenomics. Web3, for me, is decentralisation, it's openness, it's transparency."

Gavin Wood[47]

Leaders of the Web3 technology movement place a significant value on visibility and openness for future developments.

Why visibility is important

Building engagement, a motivated workforce, and optimised teams is aided through visibility. The rapid discovery and deployment of skills enables fast and balanced team formation; awareness and recognition of contribution aids the development of intrinsic motivation; while making values and processes clear helps to bring people along on the organisational journey and generates trust.

---

[47] Wood, G. (2022) *Polkadot's Gavin Wood on Building a Layer 0 to Underpin the Entire Blockchain-Based Economy*. The Defiant Podcast, YouTube

Enabling Visibility

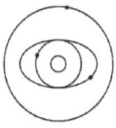

"There is an observable set of correlations that are not being considered by most governments: you need to be open to gain trust, and you need trust to get citizens fully engaged"
Government Chief Information Officer[48]

Visible processes aid the development of trust and connection and provide a range of benefits for organisations - from governments engaging with citizens to companies looking to engage with customers or a wider community.

Awareness is a key part of a mesh mindset and mesh culture as it prompts continual seeking of individual and organisational insights on which to base decisions. It is necessary for the formation of connections and information flow, in the recognition of skills and contribution, and it contributes to the development of trust and sustainability.

Making processes visible helps individuals understand how to engage, and who or what to connect with

---

[48] Hamilton, G. & Kelchner, J. (2021) *Insights Report: At the Interchange of Open Culture & Navigating Futures*. Interchange

to contribute at their best. Making skills visible aids awareness of the potential within the organisation, which assists deployment and the formation of flexible cross-functional teams, while making contribution visible helps to guard against hidden work, which can impact sustainability.

A lack of awareness of what is happening within an organisation can lead to TUV. Hidden work is a challenge for open projects, which enable people to contribute outside of formal roles, based on their interests or skills. Open projects often benefit from free contribution from individuals who wish to contribute to something meaningful, who might want to test their skills, or who are looking to build up a portfolio of evidence of open source code development to help them in their career. However, when that contribution is not formally recognised, is unpaid, or there is no longer a clear benefit to the contributor, it will inevitably make the open project unsustainable.[49] Hidden and free work presents a risk to open projects and decentralised approaches. Potential pitfalls can be addressed with a focus on contribution visibility and developing realms of awareness - self-awareness, organisational awareness and global awareness.

---

[49] Pennington, H. (2019) *Open source has a working-for-free problem.* Tidelift

Balancing varied perspectives and the needs of different communities and contexts is also important in a mesh culture. Balanced teams comprising different contribution tendencies often deliver better outcomes, while balancing input from a mix of backgrounds, perspectives and skills can lead to more considered and robust products and services. Balanced contributions in collaborative efforts provide value that aids in sustainability. All contributors add a capability that can be used to balance efforts by how they make decisions, how they respond to uncertainty, and how they influence others around them.

When choosing what is made visible, consideration must be given to differing needs and striking the right balance. While transparent processes can help build trust, unauthorised sharing of personal data to which individuals have a right to privacy, will destroy trust. Appropriate application of what to make visible and what to keep private can be thought of as dialling up and down what is shared based on context, regulation and impact on trust.

The power of emerging technologies is not restricted to their digital affordances but also lies in the concepts of openness and transparency. These have multi-dimensional significance to future developments.

Visibility is a core tenet of mesh organisations. It aids engagement and the development of trust, and helps generate a sense of shared purpose, prompting components and communities to work together towards future goals.

It needs to be balanced with awareness of context and respect for varying needs and regulatory requirements, as well as a right to privacy and user-control. When these are in place, it:

- Creates conditions for flexibility by providing people with access to information so that they can prepare for eventualities and emerging contexts.
- Helps identify skills and contributions for optimal deployment, which aids resilience.
- Yields a higher likelihood of communities engaging, forgiving mistakes and providing valuable contributions, which supports sustainability of the organisation.

Trust

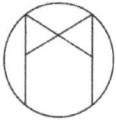

"Trust is like the air we breathe - when it's present, nobody really notices. When it's absent, everyone notices."
Warren Buffet[50]

The prominent investor, Warren Buffet, commenting on the necessity of trust for financial transactions, highlights the impact a lack of trust can have. Similarly, trust has a significant effect on organisational interactions.

Why trust is important

Performance, customer engagement and positive business relationships are empowered through trust. A culture that enables trust will empower personal agency, including psychological safety, to help individuals contribute at their best. It will also promote openness about organisational values and processes, so that customers and other

---

[50] Buffett, W. quoted in Khoury, G. & Crabtree, S. (2019) *Are businesses worldwide suffering from a trust crisis?* Gallup

stakeholders can make value-based decisions about what they invest in and what their money is helping to fund.

Enabling trust

From the perspective of how trust can positively impact the contribution of individuals in an organisation, trust is more likely to be generated when individuals are trusted to have personal agency and when they feel psychologically safe.

Psychological safety has been shown to be a key factor for enabling high-performing teams.[51] Individuals are more likely to contribute ideas when they know they are valued and they are given opportunities to experiment, to fail and explore ideas without fear of negative repercussions.[52] This helps individuals to generate value and the organisation to benefit more fully from their skills.

Trust practices can be built into organisations to empower psychological safety. Certain contexts, such as learning, the integration of new technology, or change - contexts that are often messy or chaotic - can create feelings of vulnerability. These contexts compel the exploration of ideas, making mistakes, cycling through hypotheses, iterating and questioning oneself. Specific channels or avenues to enable idea exploration, failure,

---

[51] Duhigg, C. (2016) *What Google Learned From Its Quest to Build the Perfect Team*. The New York Times
[52] Edmondson, A. (1999) *Psychological Safety and Learning Behavior in Work Teams*. Sage Publications

learning from mistakes and iteration can be provided in any type of organisation.

Trust is built into trustless organisations such as Decentralised Autonomous Organisations.[53] These enable visibility of transactions, such as in the form of smart contracts where an action is triggered automatically upon agreed conditions having been met, which could be payment by cryptocurrency into an individual's crypto wallet for example. Smart contracts negate the need for an assumption of trust that a transaction will occur at some other time or be processed through an intermediary such as a bank. Trust is built in through the visibility of the exchange.

Processes for learning from mistakes are a particular feature of high-reliability organisations, which focus on ensuring mistakes or failures are learned from and acted upon through updated practices and processes. This focus on seeing failure as a learning opportunity, and making necessary changes based on the new awareness generated from lessons learned, is a core part of what makes them high-reliability organisations, and helps to regenerate trust in the organisation.

Trust is a core tenet of mesh organisations. It helps individuals and teams to perform at their best, aids in the

---

[53] Sims, A. (2019) *Blockchain and Decentralised Autonomous Organisations (DAOs): The Evolution of Companies?* 28 New Zealand Universities Law Review 423-458

development of services and solutions that are understood through their visibility, and promotes engagement.

It needs visibility and awareness balanced with learning. When these are in place, it:

- Enables flexibility through teams empowered by psychological safety that perform well and innovate rapidly.
- Aids resilience through visibility of exchanges, interactions and transactions.
- Promotes sustainable engagement through trust regeneration from visible application of lessons learned.

Conditions

In our work with organisations, we have found that certain conditions catalyse (re)generative behaviours and processes and help optimise operations and contribution. They form the acronym ORBITALS.

ORBITALS

Open

Encompasses approaches, ways of working and cultural norms that promote adaptability, transparency, inclusivity, collaboration, and community. Openness prompts a mindset and behaviours that are beneficial for managing decentralisation, and aids organisational flexibility, resilience and sustainability.

Regeneration

Prompts a willingness to transform through continuous cycles of change, and to generate and regenerate to remain relevant and be sustainable.

Balance

Prompts balancing of different perspectives, inputs and components, such as balancing the needs of different communities and contexts, or balancing an individual's rights to privacy with the application of visibility to gain meaningful insights.

Information Flow

Empowers connection, knowledge building, decision-making, the exchange of data, ideas and information, contribution by distributed and potentially decentralised components, and engagement with communities.

Trust practices

Are key to developing sustainable relationships and partnerships, empowering teams, defining ethical behaviours and enabling good governance.

Awareness

Helps individuals and organisations understand where they are now, where they want to go and what they need to do to get there.

Learning

Aids rapid adaptation and regeneration. Connecting and weaving distributed knowledge with collaborative learning opportunities enables individuals to learn through the exchange of ideas and provides opportunities for connection, exploration and network formation.

Sustainability

Prompts consideration of all parts of the organisational mesh, including connections to the wider world and the sustainability issues concerning it - to remain relevant, be resilient and future-proof developments.

These conditions are threaded through the design, help enable the tenets of connection, visibility and trust, and help to direct the implementation of an open, regenerative culture; a flexible, mesh structure; and to maximise the opportunities of Web3.

Implementing The Design

8.

Mesh Mindsets

Mindsets

The first area we will consider for implementing the Mesh organisational design, is mindsets. We can think of mindsets as how individuals think, act and process information and change. Mindsets shape how an individual makes sense of the world and their approach to how they work. The term can also be used to describe how an organisation thinks and acts.

Learning, Evolving & Iterating

One of the practices of a mesh organisation is continual regeneration. The granular, mesh structure lends itself to small, continual iterations and lessens the disruption that can occur with transformation in fixed organisations. For example, in fixed contexts digital transformation of monolithic software can lead to significant downtime as new software is installed and members of the organisation learn how to navigate and use the extensive new software package and associated processes.

With an iterative approach, small changes become a daily occurrence and part of the usual processes of the organisation. The organisation is constantly learning and evolving based on what new insights it gains in order to improve performance and become more efficient.

This process of regeneration releases value because the organisation is continuously checking in with where it is now, where it wants to be and what tweaks it needs to make to get there. Regeneration, therefore, is a necessary part of sustainability, as the organisation navigates uncertain futures and implements new technologies. To enable regeneration:

- Individuals are prompted to adapt and flex by developing self and skills awareness and become self-directing learners to help them contribute at their best within changing circumstances.
- Individuals and the organisation must be responsive, agile and resilient while navigating change.
- The organisation must be responsive to changes in the global context, in order to remain relevant and be sustainable.

Navigating Change

In organisations with fixed, inflexible structures and processes, organisational regeneration is often disruptive and can lead to a drop in productivity and morale. In mesh organisations, change is a continual cycle of small adjustments, which is less disruptive and more manageable.

Within the evolving contexts of mesh organisations individuals need to flex and adapt to new developments. This prompts the need for a mindset that values continual development - of awareness, learning and active engagement with the process of change. Such a mindset needs to enable individuals to generate value, regenerate and evolve within the wider context of continual change.

Expanding Awareness

Change happens every moment of the day as individuals interact with their environment. As an individual engages with new information they respond and react in conscious as well as unconscious ways, with internal programming informing their behaviours.[54] If we think of the human mind as hardware that runs internal programmes based on experiences, beliefs and values, these can inadvertently

---

[54] Bargh, J.A. & Morsella, E. (2008) *The Unconscious Mind.* Perspect Psychol Sci. 2008 Jan;3(1):73-9. National Library of Medicine

create barriers and limitations. As information is processed, the individual makes decisions based on current awareness, and as new information is committed to memory, it may be generalised. When drawing on such knowledge in future, therefore, it is important for the individual to check for assumptions and understand the context in which the knowledge was first formed.

This is just one of many areas where behaviours, patterns or processes may be unclear or hidden to an individual or an organisation. A focus on continuously seeking to expand awareness provides enlightenment to individuals and the organisation, helping to shine a light on areas that are dark, to understand and take account of their behaviours and belief systems, see the unseen and develop greater insights to inform decision-making.

Understanding Contribution

Research suggests that how an individual processes information will impact how they tend or prefer to contribute.[55] Understanding contribution tendencies can be helpful for empowering people to contribute at their best because individuals are more likely to invest deeply in

---

[55] Rowe, A. J. & Boulgarides, J. D. (1992) *Managerial Decision Making*. New York: Macmillan Publishing Company

something if they are intrinsically motivated to do so.[56] [57] Being enabled to contribute in ways that they enjoy is likely to result in more engaged, productive and generative individuals.

Any consideration of contribution tendencies within a mesh context will refrain from defining fixed labels for an individual and consider a spectrum of contribution preferences or tendencies rather than absolutes. The insights generated about tendencies and preferences can be used to aid dynamic and cross-functional deployment rather than to fit individuals into fixed roles. Such understanding can help an individual and organisation gain insights on how an individual is more likely to input to problem-solving, participation and collaboration. Individuals, particularly those at the start of their working lives, can be unaware of their intrinsic motivators or core skills.[58] Helping individuals and the organisation to understand them enables individuals to contribute at their best and aids the organisation's awareness of the skills and capabilities available to it.

---

[56] Deci, E. & Ryan, R. (2000) *Intrinsic and Extrinsic Motivations: Classic Definitions and New Directions*. Contemporary Educational Psychology 25,54–67 (2000)

[57] Deci, E. & Ryan, R. (2010) *Intrinsic Motivation*. The Corsini Encyclopedia of Psychology

[58] Savitz-Romer, M & Bouffard, M. (2012) *Ready, Willing and Able. A Developmental Approach to College Access and Success*. Harvard Education Press

Mesh Mindset

A mesh mindset contains a number of other mindsets. It is informed by the mesh tenets: connection - thinking and acting in ways that promote connection and information flow; visibility - actively seeking insights to inform decision making; and trust - integrating trust practices to create generative environments. It is augmented by mindsets that aid the ability to adapt to change, compel the continual development of awareness, and prompt understanding of intrinsic motivations and contribution tendencies. We will consider how these regenerative, enlightenment and contribution mindsets might manifest through the lenses of the core, operational and global.

Core | Power Source

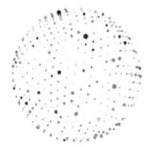

Regenerative Mindset

From a core perspective, a regenerative mindset can be thought of as how individuals and leaders engage with change through the development of awareness, the action of learning, and the process of integrating new understanding. It informs how individuals approach updating their awareness and how they experience and engage with the organisation.

A regenerative mindset encourages an individual to proactively adjust to their environment through continuous learning and the development of self-awareness. It informs learning agility and the ability to navigate uncertainty. It incorporates the understanding that intelligence and talent are malleable and can be developed.[59] A regenerative mindset enables individuals to see, think and act in ways that promote flexibility in changing environments and aids decision-making for beneficial course correction prompted by new information.

A regenerative mindset might manifest as:
- Consciously engaging with new information
- Being curious and open to exploring, failing and iterating
- Continuously considering the lessons that can be learned from experiences and from others
- Being willing to reframe identity, to change focus and direction, and to reprioritize goals
- Remaining adaptive when organising for work rather than adhering to a strict plan

---

[59] Dweck, C. (2007) *Mindset: The New Psychology of Success*. Ballantine Books

- Continuously seeking ways to improve and repurpose skills and abilities
- Valuing one's own and others' time, energy and contributions
- Respecting others' opinions, even if they do not align with one's own
- Seeking opportunities to co-create for the greater good
- Integrating information from the wider ecosystem to inform and weave into one's own work
- Recognising the need to deconstruct what one knows in order to regenerate and evolve

Enlightenment Mindset

With new information an individual creates new neural patterns and develops their capacities and capabilities.[60] An enlightenment mindset prompts an individual to expand their awareness beyond current understanding that may be limiting their capacity.

It will prompt an individual to question their own biases as well as the biases of sources of information, and consider the perspectives, beliefs or agendas influencing them. Awareness about why they think a certain way can aid

---

[60] Von Bernhardi, R. et al (2017) *What Is Neural Plasticity?*. In: von Bernhardi, R., Eugenín, J., Muller, K. (eds) The Plastic Brain. Advances in Experimental Medicine and Biology, vol 1015. Springer, Cham

enlightenment of how a perspective or belief may be blocking regeneration or trapping value.

Contribution Mindset

Understanding how an individual prefers or tends to contribute can help an organisation assign them to work that plays to their strengths, and help the individual seek work that they will enjoy and perform well. A contribution mindset prompts individuals to gain understanding of their intrinsic motivators and contribution tendencies.

Awareness of their contribution tendencies enables an individual to articulate how and where they can contribute best. When combined with nuanced awareness of skills, this information can be used to gain greater visibility of organisational capabilities to create more effective teams powered by balanced skills and contribution clusters, and to aid flexible, rapid and optimal deployment in a variety of contexts.

Operational | Power Plant

Regenerative Mindset

When an organisation has a regenerative mindset, it seeks to regenerate and adjust business to emerging environments. This mindset prompts the organisation to integrate behaviours, processes and structures that enable iterative regeneration.

From an operational perspective, regeneration can be generated through:

- Offering formal and informal opportunities for continuous learning and the development of awareness by individuals, teams and the organisation as a whole
- The cultivation of frequent dialogue and information flow about the organisation's goals and strategies
- Embracing discussions on failure and what has been learned, in order to regenerate and continuously improve
- Collective decision-making and problem-solving to yield more aligned generation and results

- Approaching developments with a collaborative mindset from the outset

Enlightenment Mindset

An enlightenment mindset prompts an organisation to expand awareness of operations, structures and emerging technologies and capabilities.

Gathering feedback and insightful data to reveal TUV can be generated through annual employee surveys and 360 reviews but insights will be significantly amplified when augmented with learning from daily conversations, project wrap-ups, open dialogue on challenges, listening to customers' pain points and following information sources on emerging technologies.

Prioritising discovery to gain organisational insights not only helps reveal areas where value is trapped or untapped but can aid in reducing disruptions and helping the organisation to maintain business relevance.

Making the unseen visible empowers navigation through uncertainty and minimises barriers to expansion. Web3 technology and increased access to data sources means there are more opportunities than ever to develop nuanced insights, which may be drawn from contribution patterns, conversations, feedback loops, collaborative sessions, and a variety of other internal and external data sources.

Contribution Mindset

Organisational operations power the gathering, generation and distribution of collective contributions. Awareness of contributions is critical to effective operations, and balanced contribution clusters (teams) optimise productivity and organisational outputs.

A mesh organisation focuses on enlightening itself, and as such aims to know the contribution tendencies of the individuals within it, has clear rules for participation and provides conduits for contribution across the organisation.

Generating the awareness required to create balanced teams is aided through asking questions. The following provide examples of where different contribution tendencies would be preferable depending on the response:

- Do we need analysis of details and to identify risks, or to envisage innovative ways for the business to reinvent itself?
- Do we need to manage uptake and gather feedback, or a strategy for engagement to foster connection and build community?
- Are we seeking to maintain a process or to develop new processes for growth and sustainability?

The answers to questions such as these will help to identify individuals with the most relevant contribution tendencies for the type of output - innovators or maintainers, preferences for the microcosm or the macrocosm, and so on.

Global | Power Broker

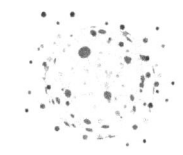

Regenerative Mindset

The interface between the external ecosystem, conceptualised as a power broker, and the organisation influences how the value of the organisation is distributed and engaged with. Consideration of the global context helps an organisation to regenerate to remain relevant and to tap into new and valuable markets.

From a global perspective, regeneration can be generated by:

- Awareness and understanding of key concerns and themes of external communities and stakeholders that are important to the organisation
- Using awareness about these external concerns and themes to inform decision-making and course-correction

Enlightenment Mindset

A mesh organisation seeks to understand how external stakeholders, such as existing and potential customers, view it, where their blocks to engagement might lie, and what they value.

Awareness might be generated by:

- Leveraging external data sources to identify TUV to improve service levels and build better solutions
- Understanding perception of the impact the organisation has on the planet and society
- Listening to topics of interest from different demographics to understand and build engagement

Contribution Mindset

A mesh organisation recognises that circumstances evolve. It seeks to continuously understand current and future skills and contribution needs and to develop conduits for bringing new skills and contribution into the organisation.

External data sources can provide useful insights of current and projected skills gaps. Clustering this with data on the contribution tendencies and skills within the organisation, empowers an organisation to make better informed decisions about interventions it can take to ensure optimal productivity and sustained operations.

Making this information visible and shareable, such as through digital open recognition of skills, would release value not only to the organisation but to the wider ecosystem, and could aid identification of opportunities for open contribution and collaboration beyond the organisational borders.

9.
Mesh | Core

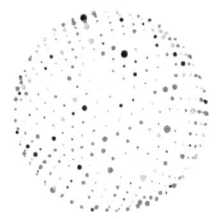

Core - The Power Source

At the core of a mesh organisation is the leadership team, which we conceptualise as the power source. It is the job of the leadership team to create a generative environment to power productivity through high morale and agency.

In our conceptual model, we envisage the core as a sun-like orb at the heart of the organisation, that provides power, direction and warmth to energise and empower the surrounding mesh.

Leadership

In reality, it is formed of a generative group of leaders that empower generative people and are comfortable with navigating regeneration. Such leaders will inspire and surface the intrinsic motivation of all members of the organisation and empower high performance through personal agency and by creating a psychologically safe environment with channels for innovation and growth. The leadership team see themselves as a core part of the organisational mesh, leading from the centre, and acting as bridgemakers to form connections. In the mesh, information flows in all directions, enabling continual regeneration throughout the organisation.

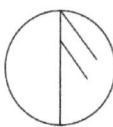

People have the highest capacity for generating value in an organisation.

Core human capabilities such as empathy, agency and those feelings we might call intuition or a gut feeling, make people highly generative beings. In a world of AI and bots, people are able to flex and adapt in a way that machines have to be programmed to do.

However, as we discussed in the chapter on TUV, there are many ways in which the generative and regenerative value of people can be restricted. Things like lack of connection to others or to the purpose of the organisation, lack of visibility and recognition of contribution or skills, and a lack of trust will quickly trap the extent of the value individuals can bring to the organisation, resulting in untapped potential.

Self-awareness

Core can also be applied to any individual in the organisation in reference to their core beliefs and mindsets. Self-awareness describes an individual's understanding of themselves and their awareness about how they individually impact and respond to developments.

Self-awareness helps individuals understand their motivations, concerns and skills, including their core human capabilities. By focusing on developing self-awareness individuals can begin to identify what restricts them adding value to the organisation, such as unarticulated skills. Knowledge of what might trap the value they could bring, and the ability to identify value that is untapped can help individuals determine relevant opportunities to help them contribute at their best, and to become self-regulating and generative members of the organisation.

Developing a mesh mindset will aid the development of self-awareness and other practices that help optimise an individual's contribution.

Enabling the Tenets

Using the core lens we can look at how the tenets of connection, visibility and trust might manifest through certain practices.

Connection

When individuals connect, they share their ideas and skills through exchange. Collaborators and communities connect around a common purpose united by shared values and goals. Thinking and behaviours when connecting are impacted by an individual's sense of psychological safety and their preparedness to share, to collectively generate ideas, purpose and outputs.

By using connection practices individuals are prompted to see, think and act in ways that promote connection, value contributions, seek out diverse perspectives, enable information flow across all parts of the ecosystem and encourage participation to create stronger outputs together.

Connection practices can manifest as:
- Inviting input for collective development
- Creating & catalysing connections that produce creative work
- Empowering agency for building of connections and networks across teams
- Assuming, for the most part, that collective outputs will outperform individual outputs
- Actively pursuing varied perspectives
- Creating a shared sense of identity and mission
- Committing to collective rules, common standards and etiquettes
- Aiming for consensus-based decision making, where feasible
- Assembling multi-disciplinary teams
- Leading with empathy and high emotional intelligence to build strong relationships
- Building community with intention and recognising contributions
- Encapsulating context and nuance when communicating and directing others
- Expressing the dynamics of relationships between the parts of the whole organisation and identifying multiple perspectives
- Modelling communication standards for the community

- Facilitating conversations and collaboration as a bridgemaker to bring others along on the journey
- Considering the needs for expanded coordination of collaborative efforts

Visibility

Visibility is vital for decision making, solution development, relational connection, and engagement. By using visibility practices, individuals are prompted to see, think and act in ways that promote visibility, make intentions and expectations clear, and enhance information flow.

Visibility practices can manifest as:
- Clearly communicating expectations
- Being honest about how things work
- Being open and clear about the mission, goal, 'the why'
- Providing clarity and context about problems and challenges
- Being open about mistakes and limitations as well as strengths and successes
- Actively pursuing hard conversations
- Being willing to share knowledge and work with others
- Recognising the varied ways individuals contribute to the success of the organisation

- Exploring data to identify patterns and form connections from collective intelligence
- Seeing the macro view to understand the functioning of the wider organisation, its interactions and interconnectedness
- Navigating change with understanding of context

Trust

Trust creates a generative environment for ideas, engagement and sense of ownership in work. Trust flourishes when individuals feel valued for their contributions, and when different backgrounds and voices are recognised for the value their diverse perspectives can bring. By using trust practices individuals are prompted to see, think and act in ways that promote trust, visible exchanges, information flow and a sense of belonging.

Trust practices can manifest as:
- Modelling shared values and principles
- Ensuring individuals feel valued for their contributions
- Taking ownership of one's words and actions
- Valuing diversity of perspective and thought
- Empowering individuals to contribute to the best of their abilities

- Including individuals in decision-making
- Ensuring individuals feel psychologically safe
- Empowering personal agency
- Encouraging individuals and communities to explore possibilities
- Seeking consent to ensure boundaries are held and to initiate ethical sharing of information and practices
- Creating communities and connections that hold value for members
- Shaping practices and systems that empower equity
- Articulating clear goals and boundaries for scope of work and decision-making

10.
Mesh | Operational

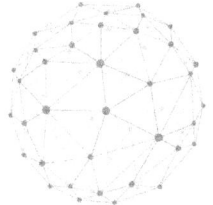

Operational - The Power Plant

The operational component of a mesh organisation is conceptualised as the power plant. These are the individuals, teams, technology, data and other components that power and deliver the work of the organisation.

In our conceptual model, we envisage this as an orb-like mesh that surrounds the core, and which is made up of distributed nodes (components) that are connected to form a network that conducts information. Organisational clusters within the mesh (teams, projects, communities and related organisations) also coalesce around their own core and form their own mesh. Like fractals, mesh organisations have a similar structure in the micro (teams, projects, communities and related organisations) and the macro (the whole organisation).

Operationalising the Mesh

Operationalising the mesh requires that existing and new nodes - the various components that make up an organisation including people, technology and data - can connect in a way that lets the organisation flex, adapt and scale. The structure of the mesh enables organisations to add and tap into multiple, changeable, potentially distributed components, which in turn provide evolving opportunities to help reveal what is unseen and release value.

Organisational Awareness

Organisational awareness prompts leaders to check if processes promote or prevent optimal contribution and use of the value available to it, and to identify what needs to change in order to do so. Developing organisational awareness, gaining insights and gathering data from the various components within the organisation can help leaders identify TUV and release it for organisational benefit.

A mesh mindset will help the organisation focus on behaviours and practices that optimise processes and contribution within the organisation.

Structure

A mesh organisation functions in a number of different ways to a non-mesh organisation, which for our purposes, we will refer to as mesh or fixed processes.

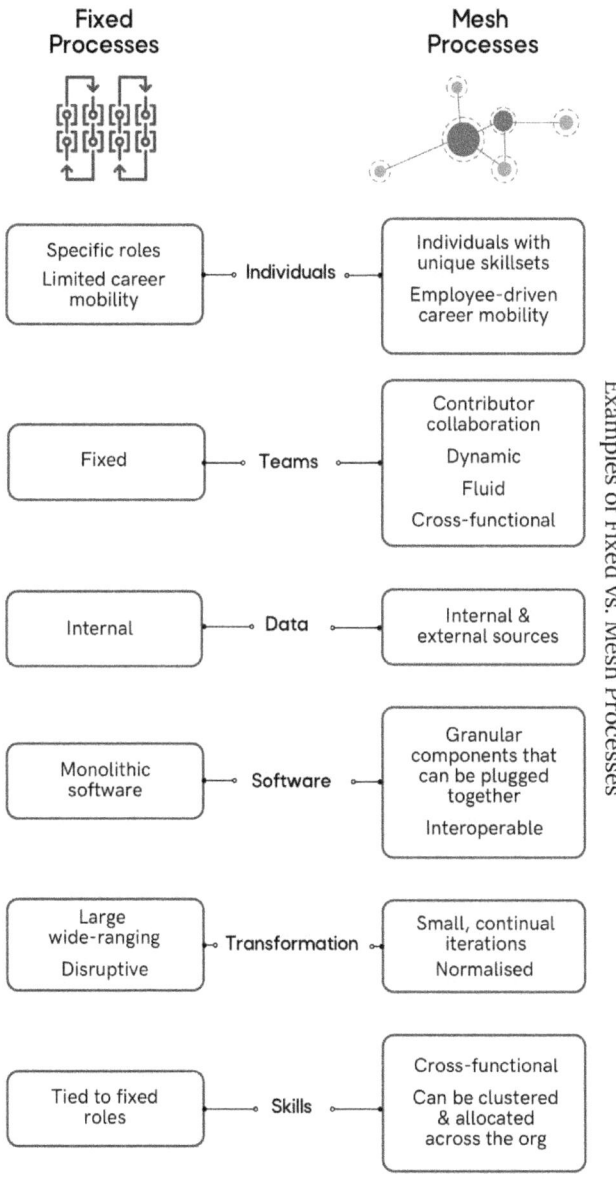

Examples of Fixed vs. Mesh Processes

Enabling the Tenets

There are many ways the tenets of connection, visibility and trust might manifest from an operations perspective. The following are a few examples.

Connection

From an operations perspective, connection can be generated through:

- Processes for enabling information flow across the organisation, for sharing stories and building collective knowledge
- Hosting channels for cross-organisational interactions, online and in-person (if possible)
- Enabling individuals to work and engage with others in ways that align with their communication preferences, as far as feasible
- Clearly defined common 'languages'
- Cross-functional & multi-disciplinary teams
- Coordination of collaboration with governance that scales with demand
- Networks of support across teams and disciplines
- Using Web3 granular and interoperable technologies that can be easily added to, managed and removed

Visibility

From an operations perspective, visibility can be generated through:

- Recognising skills and contribution in a digital, granular and shareable way so that the data can be drawn on and clustered to provide visibility in a variety of areas, to be used for deployment, understanding future skills needs and so on
- Clearly articulating values, expected cultural practices and structural processes and making this information easily discoverable
- Processes to regularly discuss failure, what has been learned and to celebrate successes
- Providing access to information, particularly to leaders for insights into the whole organisational system
- Ensuring projects and organisational work is visible to avoid duplication and enable beneficial connections to be made for learning and outputs
- Sharing work early and often
- Using Web3 enabled visualisation tools to draw on a variety of internal and external data sources that can be clustered and re-clustered to generate different insights

Trust

From an operations perspective, trust can be generated through:

- Deployment, skills and learning programmes that empower individuals to develop their skillsets and identify opportunities to contribute at their best
- Structured processes for collective decision-making, problem-solving and feedback
- Providing psychologically safe spaces and opportunities for ideation and learning
- Catering for cognitive diversity and diversity of backgrounds, education, thinking and communication styles
- Continually gathering and assessing insights and sharing information about changes made to act on lessons learned
- Developing processes and governance for exploring possibilities
- Making the whole organisation's goals and initiatives accessible to enable system-thinking and integrated development
- Using Web3 technologies such as smart contracts, tokens and blockchains for trustless task-based contracts and value exchange

11.
Mesh | Global

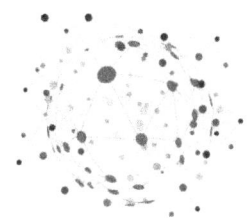

Global - The Power Broker

The global component of a mesh organisation is thought of conceptually as the power broker. These are the distributed and external stakeholders and communities that engage across and with the organisation.

In our conceptual model, we envisage the global as components that orbit the organisation and organisational clusters within the mesh that are drawn in by gravitational pull. It also refers to the wider ecosystem that the organisation is situated within.

Global

Mesh organisations thrive through extending their connections and consciousness to encompass wider, external sources. To misquote John Donne's meditations in 1624 on connectedness...

No organisation is an island

In the powerful poem still regularly quoted to this day, Donne mused that "no man is an island" and that our empathy and consciousness should extend beyond ourselves.[61] The pertinence for our purpose is that there is value in our connections. Being able to capitalise on the wealth of knowledge and value others can bring, is part of the strength of a mesh organisation. The external and global components of customers, communities and other external stakeholders and data, have a brokering impact on the organisation, being influenced by it and in turn influencing perception and engagement with it.

---

[61] Donne, J. (1624) MEDITATION XVII. *Devotions upon Emergent Occasions.*

Tapping into a global network of people and data helps organisations develop resilience through understanding and cultivation of positive perception, sustainability through awareness of the collective consciousness, and the flexibility to benefit from opportunities for expansion from new external sources.

Global Awareness

Global awareness encourages consideration of the key concerns and values of the wider community, their perception of, and engagement with the organisation, and what actions would increase positive engagement from customers and other stakeholders.

A mesh mindset will help the organisation focus on behaviours and practices that aid external engagement and perception.

Enabling the Tenets

From a global perspective the tenets of connection, visibility and trust might manifest in the following ways.

Connection

From a global perspective, connection can be generated by:

- Connections with external communities, encouraging them to engage and feel part of the journey
- Partnerships and support ecosystems that can provide diverse perspectives and inputs
- Enabling stakeholders to align with the organisation through bridgemaking, shared language and by negotiating clear outcomes
- Open collaboration with distributed contributors
- Joint experiences based around projects, learning and social connection
- Governance and systems for recognition of community contributions
- Processes and support for consensus-based decision-making, inputs and feedback
- Pathways for leaders to facilitate bridgemaking conversations with the wider, external ecosystem

Visibility

From a global perspective, visibility can be generated by:
- Open, co-creation design events
- Making key developments visible for community consideration and input
- Seeking insights from communities and external stakeholders about their needs now and for the future
- Drawing upon the expertise and knowledge of stakeholders when making decisions and gathering feedback
- Communicating in different ways and through a variety of channels, respecting the needs and preferences of different community demographics
- Using Web3 technologies to gather data on blocks to uptake to develop a more productive and seamless customer and stakeholder journey
- Using collective data to identify patterns and employ systems thinking to inform solution design and development

Trust

From a global perspective, trust can be generated by:
- Sharing the values of the organisation's cultural and structural practices

- Being honest with customers, stakeholders and external communities about mistakes and successes, and sharing lessons learned
- Being intentional about what to share, and balancing visibility with consideration of regulations and privacy
- Using Web3 technologies that enable transparent interactions and transactions to help stakeholders understand how the organisation behaves and what their money is helping to fund
- Governance that states clear boundaries and ethical practices for information gathering and sharing
- Intentional community building governance that adds value and empowers equity building
- Scaling for decentralised activities and democratic decision-making

Powering Performance

12.

Empowering (Re)Generative People

Powering Performance

People are an organisation's most generative asset. Organisational practices that devalue people will burn out individuals and damage the organisation's income generating capabilities.

In this chapter we will explore in more detail, some of the ways in which organisations can empower people in ways that enrich the individual and the organisation. We will explore this from an individual, team and global perspective and consider: personal agency; psychological safety; lifelong learning; high-performing teams; human-centricity; collaboration over competition; creating networks; advocates and ambassadors; and sustaining and regenerating.

Empowering (Re)Generative People

Processes and practices can block or enable the generative potential of individuals, teams and communities. Value can become trapped or remain untapped in each of these contexts, which will inhibit an organisation's ability to optimise the value that exists within it or benefit from value that it can tap into.

We will consider how organisations can release this value through empowering generative people.

Individual

Personal Agency

Personal agency can be thought of as having a sense of agency and ownership of one's work, and a belief that "I am the cause of my own thoughts and actions".[62] Personal agency is driven by the belief individuals have in themselves to exercise control over their own functioning. An individual's self-efficacy (a facet of personal agency) regulates how they function and impacts cognitive, motivational, emotional, and choice processes.[63]

Abraham Maslow's renowned theory of human motivation and hierarchy of needs, suggests that motivations for agency are an individual's desire to expand themselves, to achieve and to make a mark.[64] Individual's feel compelled to apply their knowledge, talents and capabilities and this

---

[62] Bandura, A. (1982) *Self-efficacy mechanism in human agency*. American psychologist

[63] Bandura, A. (2001) *Social Cognitive Theory and Clinical Psychology*. International Encyclopedia of Social & Behavioral Sciences. 2001, p. 14250-14254. Pergamon

[64] Maslow, A.H. (1954) *Motivation and personality*. Harpers

prompts them to self-direct and self-develop for personal and professional growth.

When personal agency is inhibited, through micro-management for example, it can lead to self-doubt and feelings that personal growth is being stifled. Personal agency, therefore, is important for motivating individuals to contribute at their best and empowering them to generate optimal value.

Psychological Safety

Comprehensive studies have shown that the most important indicator for high-performing teams is psychological safety.[65] [66] Psychological safety can be considered to exist when the individuals within the team feel valued for the unique perspectives and experiences they bring. When individuals trust that they are safe to explore ideas and solutions, the team will fail faster, iterate and develop innovative, robust solutions more rapidly.

Psychological safety helps to release the value of the skills and contribution tendencies of individuals in an organisation, and can be enabled by team processes and leadership that include and recognise individuals for the unique value they bring. Individuals can also take personal

---

[65] Edmondson, A. (1999) *Psychological Safety and Learning Behavior in Work Teams*. Sage Publications
[66] Duhigg, C. (2016) *What Google Learned From Its Quest to Build the Perfect Team*. The New York Times

accountability for it by developing awareness of their own behaviours and needs, while balancing consideration of these with those of others.

A sense of ownership and being trusted to get on with the job contributes to feelings of psychological safety, motivating individuals to invest in their work. Clarity about expectations, how to contribute and where to find relevant help and resources, enables individuals to rapidly and effectively contribute even in new and evolving circumstances.

Lifelong Learning

Continuous learning helps individuals to regenerate and adapt to changing circumstances. Learning new skills and learning from what did and did not work helps individuals increase awareness about their skills and patterns of behaviour. It can help them determine what they could improve and what they enjoy. This knowledge can help them to contribute more effectively.[67]

Mesh organisations provide time and space for individuals to engage in learning opportunities. It is unrealistic to expect individuals to produce 100% of their time at work and to engage in learning activities beneficial to the organisation only in their own time. Learning is an active

---

[67] Dweck, C. (2007) *Mindset: The New Psychology of Success*. Ballantine Books

process and can be challenging as well as ultimately rewarding. It requires conscious thought and space to be able to fully engage with new concepts and to meaningfully incorporate the lessons into personal behaviours and actions.

While time and space is needed for reflection and other learning activities, not all learning has to be delivered through formal means, however, such as courses or training workshops. Providing opportunities for individuals to connect with other teams, other areas of expertise, and internal and external communities will help individuals learn, gain understanding of other perspectives in the context of the organisational mission, and develop skill in systems thinking. This kind of situational learning needs to be consciously enabled by the organisation, and encouragement to engage in these types of informal learning opportunities help to not only increase the learning and understanding of the individual but also forge flexible networks of connected individuals and enable information flow. When such connections already exist, skills can be more seamlessly plugged into other teams and contexts and cross-functional teams are enabled.

Teams

High-performing teams

The ability to try out ideas, fail, and iterate are key factors for innovation. The rapid pace of innovation in the open source technology sector in the first two decades of the 21st Century, demonstrated how failing early and often is better than investing years in developing something that doesn't respond to the needs of the users when launched.[68] Agile approaches, where ideas are explored, co-created and tested in rapid cycles, enable teams to learn fast and develop resilient solutions that are more likely to meet users' needs and preferences.

We have explored how psychological safety is an important factor in optimising an individual's contribution within a team. When individuals feel valued and know that their contribution is recognised and appreciated, they feel safe and motivated to contribute at their best. In mesh organisations, an individual's uniqueness is recognised and it

---

[68] Whitehurst, J. (2015) *The Open Organization: Igniting Passion and Performance.* Harvard Business Review Press

is understood that individuals respond differently to situations, contexts and communication formats when collaborating as part of a team.

Each individual has varying levels of comfort with different communication formats. An individual with valuable skills to offer an initiative may not share their opinions with the loudest voice but prefer to contribute by text, or may need time to reflect rather than launching into a fast-paced mind-mapping session. Making it clear that everyone's voice is valued and providing choices for how to communicate and connect helps cater for neurodiversity and individual communication preferences and needs.

Human-centricity

Individuals are more likely to contribute at their best when they feel valued for the human beings that they are. It may seem an obvious statement but people differ from the automatons, AI or bots that can now do some of the work of organisations because they have feelings - emotions and concerns - about their lives outside of the work of the organisation. Inevitably these occupy their thought processes while they are engaging in the work of the organisation as well as when they are not, and this will be exacerbated by financial insecurity.

Organisations going through highly disruptive restructuring do not get the best out of their employees because inevitably individuals will be spending some of their time thinking about their basic survival needs. Predictably people will be concerned about where the money will come from if their job ends, how they will fare if they have to re-apply for their job or what it will mean to work with a new boss and team.[69]

Some of these concerns can be allayed by mesh structures, where flexible processes and small iterations are the rule, rather than extensive, disruptive changes. Another way to help individuals address uncertainty, however, is through one of the things that organisations often do not want to do for fear that individuals will immediately 'jump ship'. Including individuals in decisions and discussing possible future directions for the organisation that will directly impact them, helps them plan for their futures. This helps individuals feel more in control of their career and financial concerns, which rather than prompting immediate exit is more likely to result in higher productivity because the kind of worried and looping internal conversations that arise at such times will be reduced. Reducing financial uncertainty is likely to yield more productive and generative behaviours.

---

[69] Maslow, A.H. (1954) *Motivation and personality*. Harpers

Collaboration Over Competition

While competition can be a motivating factor for many individuals, within a mesh organisation collaboration is rated higher. The ability to collaborate will help an organisation to endlessly regenerate and draw on a pool of new and re-purposed skills to meet new challenges. Ego-based competition in this context, can detract from the ability to collaborate, as individuals compete with each other for recognition for their contribution, rather than focusing on generating the best outputs for the team or organisation.

Research has shown that open source software, created through the inputs of many and often distributed individuals, can be more robust and secure than proprietary software that has been developed by a small, fixed group of individuals in a single team or company.[70] More perspectives, skillsets and areas of expertise help develop the software and put it through rigorous cycles of ideation, critique, feedback and development as each input is added.

In order for this type of collaborative effort to yield useful results, however, collaborative behaviours are essential. If individuals compete to call-out their input, perhaps by trying to minimise or even disrupt the input of others, it will diminish the overall results. The same situation can occur where individuals, ostensibly collaborating, will

---

[70] Sidhpurwala, H. (2022) *The art and science of secure open source software development.* Red Hat

not share ideas for fear of them being 'stolen' and passed off by others as their own, or because they might be used in some way to help the other individual 'get ahead'. Similarly, when individuals feel afraid to speak up and share their ideas for fear of negative repercussions, in other words when their sense of psychological safety is jeopardised, they are less likely to contribute what could have been a valuable idea to the team. When collaboration is enabled through practices and processes that recognise and value every contribution, competition is less likely and a team's generative capabilities to deliver value is enhanced.

Global

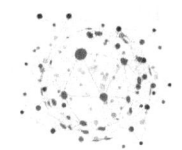

Creating Networks

For organisations to gain the most from the assets at their disposal and from those that they might tap into, they need to be able to create networks and forge connections. Structured opportunities for developing networks, collaboration and information flow can help to release the potential value present in an organisation and foster successful collaboration across and beyond it, extending who can positively contribute to the success of the organisation.

When collaboration with extended networks becomes a useful approach for an organisation, working to common standards will aid that work. Standards enable distributed developments to occur in parallel but be connected in ways that empower discovery, flexible pathways and information flow.

There are numerous ways to create networks and making a conscious choice to provide opportunities for network creation, can yield fast results. Networks might be created through focus groups, or collaborative design workshops with internal or external stakeholders. Such activities provide opportunities for not only discussing ideas and topics pertinent to the work of the organisation, but allow new connections to join the mesh and establish and extend the reach of the organisation. These connections provide the opportunity for as yet unknown value, such as skills, perspectives, or potential contributors, to be connected into the organisation and be tapped into as relevant.

Advocates & Ambassadors

Beyond the organisational mesh lies a world of potential customers, service users, citizens and other potential stakeholders for an organisation. Their perception of the organisation will provide compelling reasons as to whether they will or will not engage with it. Awareness and perception of an organisation can be addressed in a number of ways and until quite recently, it has been the domain of marketing departments to influence how others perceive the organisation.

This has changed with the rise of social media and with the increase in potential customers making value-based decisions about what organisations they do or do not want to do business with.[71] In this context, the tenets of

---

[71] PWC. (2022) *Global Consumer Insights Pulse Survey June 2022*. PWC

connection, visibility and trust play a significant role in influencing those perceptions of the organisation. Empowering people to be organisational advocates and ambassadors requires clarity about what they can share and not being too specific about what they should share. Dictated messaging lacks the individual's voice, rendering it inauthentic sounding - something that will be picked up by those engaging with it. However, with a lack of clarity about the kind of content the organisation deems acceptable to share externally, there is a tendency not to share anything at all rather than inadvertently share something potentially damaging.

Happy people are more likely to spread positive messages, and individuals that feel valued, included and recognised for their contributions, are more likely to feel happy at their work. Advocates and ambassadors may also be external stakeholders, who can help to build trusted positive perceptions. Connection, visibility and trust can manifest through the positive experiences individuals have with the organisation as a member of a wider network, or through the visibility of processes that help individuals feel confident that values such as honesty and fairness are upheld by the organisation. Individuals internal and external to the organisation can become ambassadors for it, helping to extend its reach and helping it to tap into value from the wider community.

Sustaining & Regenerating

Learning, a key part of mesh organisations, is also a feature of high-reliability organisations (HIROs) where safety is paramount. The aviation industry is a prime example of a sector replete with HIROs, where lessons are learned by organisations across the sector following an incident or accident incurred by a single organisation, usually an airline. An investigation and subsequent report will highlight what could be improved in future, and might encompass recommendations for crew resource management by the pilots, changes to organisational processes by the airline, or improvements to aspects of a plane's design by a manufacturing company.[72]

Such investigations and reports will often result in recommendations or statements to the entire sector, to help it improve and increase the safety of the industry. This has a positive impact on the commercial interests of every part of the sector because it helps to regenerate trust after an incident. While the incident cannot be changed, knowing that the sector has learned from it helps potential customers feel safe to fly again.

---

[72] Mentour Pilot. https://mentourpilot.com

Mesh organisations are informed by a regenerative mindset, where learning results in increased awareness and where insights that will lead to improvements, are acted upon.

Mesh organisations are informed by a regenerative mindset, where learning results in increased awareness and where insights that will lead to improvements, are acted upon. Such organisations are helped to become self-sustaining because they are also supported by a combination of practices and processes that empower people, through enabling personal agency, psychological safety, inclusion, networks, lifelong learning and continual generation and regeneration.

In the next chapter, we will explore how the ability to see the unseen also contributes to the sustainability and regeneration of mesh organisations, through ensuring that the most relevant skills can be discovered and deployed to release and optimise value for the organisation.

Seeing The Unseen

13.

Skills Visibility

Seeing the Unseen

Black outs on aspects of an organisation's operations will affect its ability to maximise sales revenue and optimise operations.

In this chapter we will go into some detail on an area where there is often limited visibility but where we think organisations can release significant value - skills. We will explore this from an individual, team and global perspective and consider: skills awareness; articulation; personalised pathways; cross-functional individuals; recruitment and skills discovery; retention; skills conduits; harder-to-reach groups; and skills networks.

We will finish with an overview of other instances where things may be unseen, or challenging to see, which we will address further in the chapter on Web3 solutions.

How and where learning and skills are recognised began to change at the start of the 21st century after centuries of being siloed inside formal education and delivered in a fairly linear fashion. Open education principles and open recognition standards now enable learning to be packaged and presented in a more granular way and empower personalised learning pathways. Big data and machine learning also contribute to a new landscape in which learning that happens anywhere, anytime can be collated, evidenced, assessed and recognised.

There are a number of reasons why it is useful for organisations to gain more nuanced visibility of skills. We will focus on how skills visibility can impact individuals, teams and the whole organisation. Value can become trapped or remain untapped in each of these contexts, which will inhibit an organisation's ability to optimise the value of the skills that exist within it or benefit from valuable expertise that it can tap into externally.

We will consider how organisations can release this value through skills visibility.

Skills Visibility

Individual

Skills Awareness

Developing skills awareness is useful for an individual because it can help them make career choices they will find satisfying. Helping individuals to make such choices is beneficial to organisations also because individuals are more likely to work hard and overcome obstacles for something they enjoy doing.[73][74] Choosing learning and career pathways based on intrinsic motivation is more likely to result in deeper investment in excelling in that area. Intrinsic motivation (doing something because it is enjoyed) is more likely to result in someone staying the course than extrinsic motivation (doing something purely to gain an external reward such as money or prestige).

---

[73] Deci, E. & Ryan, R. (2000) *Intrinsic and Extrinsic Motivations: Classic Definitions and New Directions.* Contemporary Educational Psychology 25,54–67 (2000)

[74] Deci, E. & Ryan, R. (2010) *Intrinsic Motivation.* The Corsini Encyclopedia of Psychology

However, not everyone finds it easy to identify their skills, particularly at the start of a career. Cultural norms and tools that help individuals become aware of their skills through the identification of patterns through a mixture of data inputs, will help individuals and the organisation see the range of skills, attributes and capacities they have. This can help individuals manage their learning and career trajectories and help organisations release the value of the skills they have at their disposal.

Skills Articulation

In 2011, the digital, open recognition standard, Open Badges, was created, which started a movement that enabled individuals to evidence, share and control their learning and achievements, gained across formal and informal contexts.[75] Open Badges provided an infrastructure for verifiable digital credentials to be created and issued by any individual or organisation, such as private companies, voluntary organisations, formal education institutions or civic organisations.

One of the benefits of digital recognition is the potential for including and clustering various sources of evidence of learning gained in a range of contexts. Evidence might include a video demonstrating a skill gained in the

---

[75] The Mozilla Foundation, et al. (2012) *Open Badges for Lifelong Learning*. Mozilla Foundation

workplace, or endorsements from a range of audiences, such as peers, educators and employers. These help to create a more comprehensive picture of an individual's skills and attributes than can be provided by a single academic transcript. Data-rich and situationally authentic evidence lends itself to the recognition of less tangible skills or character attributes, sometimes referred to as soft skills, that are highly sought after by employers such as empathy, curiosity, being an effective team player and so on.

Having the ability to articulate skills, assert a competency and provide the evidence to back it up can help learners refine their understanding of their skills, and help organisations discover the best 'skills-to-person' fit for their context.

Personalised Skills Pathways

Open recognition standards and digital presentation of learning provides a digital way to signpost learning activities, outline the evidence required to demonstrate the learning, and provide recognition of the learning. Digital and granular presentation of learning and skills means they can be searched for and found, connected into pathways and shared.

When granular learning, skills and credentials are connected into destination-based pathways they create stepping stones towards a goal, providing the means to move towards that destination.[76] Presented in a clear pathway to an opportunity, they can help learners see a goal and how to work towards it.

Interest-based pathways can help individuals explore what ignites their passion and aid discovery by showing possible job or career choices that stem from a particular skill. Such insights enable individuals to make more nuanced career decisions and more targeted job searches. They can also support individuals and organisations to gain better understanding of intrinsic motivations and help inform decisions about the best people to allocate to a team or project.

---

[76] Casilli, C. (2013) *Badge pathways: part 0, the prequel*. Persona Blog

Team

Cross-Functional Individuals

In some organisations, individuals are allocated to roles that are rigidly defined. Working outside of these roles is not encouraged and might be referred to as someone 'acting outside their pay grade'. When we consider the value that an individual will bring when they are working on something they feel passionately about and are particularly good at though, what benefit is there in organisational structures or cultural norms that block that?

While the idea of rigid and inflexible roles is quite entrenched, mesh organisations do not view individuals or their skillsets in such an inflexible manner. In the granular, flexible structure of a mesh organisation, skills are seen as components. By looking at skills in this more granular way, it is possible to identify the person or people who have the most relevant set of skills and are the most suited for any given project. Being able to discover skills enables rapid and flexible team formation - individuals can be allocated based on skills and passions rather than set roles.

Recruitment - Skills Discovery

In order to deploy the most appropriate individual for a project in this way, nuanced skills discovery is vital. This is where tools such as skills profiles and dashboards are useful to a mesh organisation.

As well as hard skills, skills such as resilience, empathy, agency, emotional intelligence, agility, self-reliance, the ability to communicate and navigate change, are increasingly important to organisations given the current fast pace of change. Most of these skills are not easy to assess in a traditional education or exam context, and benefit from assessment and verification across a range of real-world contexts. Digital evidence of skills, gathered across informal and formal sources, with contextualising data such as qualitative endorsements from peers or employers, helps with the verification and recognition of a range of skills.

Skills profiles can help individuals and organisational leaders identify and deploy skills. Data collated from a variety of sources, mined, parsed and used to create skills clusters, can provide beneficial insights to optimise recruitment, and skills discovery and deployment.

Retention

Attrition and high turnover is expensive, particularly for traditional and hybrid organisations with substantial proportions of full-time staff. The costs of marketing, hiring and onboarding new staff are significant.[77] In addition, it can be difficult to assess the full extent of the loss of skills when an individual leaves an organisation or how their leaving impacts the networks they had formed across the organisation and how that might impact the morale of others they connected with.

Numerous studies have found that people are more likely to commit to an organisation if they feel valued, invested in and have opportunities to grow.[78] Encouraging and providing opportunities for learning is one way to demonstrate that investment. While there is a risk that individuals will take the learning and move elsewhere to progress their career, this is less likely to occur in an organisation where they feel recognised and valued for their skills, and where they can see continual opportunities to grow and use their skills in new and satisfactory ways.[79]

---

[77] Agovino, T. (2019) *To Have and to Hold*. SHRM
[78] Gloat (2021) *Great Resignation Research Report*. Gloat
[79] Parker, S.K. & Menasce-Horowitz, J. (2022) *Majority of workers who quit a job in 2021 cite low pay, no opportunities for advancement, feeling disrespected*. Pew Research

Continual learning is part of a mesh mindset and mesh organisations enable the reuse and repurposing of skills through skills visibility and skill-based deployment.

Global

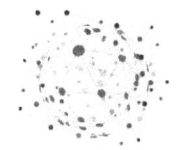

Skills Conduits

Learner demographics have changed since the 20th Century. 'Working learners' and 'learning workers' now exceed the number of 'traditional students' in the U.S.A. (i.e. those studying full-time, without full-time jobs).[80] A range of factors are affecting people's desire to follow a traditional degree, leading learners to take more control of their learning pathways. Reasons for this shift include cost, student loan debt, perceived value and the fact that some employers are moving away from degree requirements.

---

[80] Innovate+Educate (2019) *Shift Happens 2*. Innovate+Educate

Having started issuing digital micro-credentials in earnest in 2015, by 2019 IBM had issued two million of their own micro-credentials in 195 countries.[81] Industry is increasingly looking beyond traditional learning pathways to develop rapid skills conduits and ensure the skills they will need in future will be catered for.

Many world-leading companies now provide their own credentials for the core competencies they require. Micro-credentials provide faster and more flexible ways of presenting learning and recognition than traditional multi-year degrees, and organisations are increasingly seeing the opportunities they provide to get the right skills, in the right place, at the right time.[82]

---

[81] IBM (2019) *Do digital badges really provide value to businesses?* IBM
[82] Innovate+Educate (2019) *Shift Happens* 2. Innovate+Educate

Reaching Harder to Reach Groups

Research shows that young people can face significant challenges when making decisions about their future, many of which have a socio-economic basis.[83] Young people, particularly those from disadvantaged backgrounds, can struggle to articulate their strengths and often lack awareness of, and confidence in, their ability to attain a range of potentially fulfilling and rewarding career or learning opportunities. As a result, they often fail to engage with opportunities that could ultimately enhance and enrich their lives.[84]

Expectations (based on aspects of identity formed from a range of factors, including social and economic, e.g. peer group behaviours and family history) that do not support career aspirations, can result in the belief that the individual is not able to attain what they aspire to.[85]

To maximise skills conduits, therefore, it is important to enable individuals to discover learning and career opportunities, help them build the confidence to engage with them and support them to move towards them.

---

[83] Savitz-Romer, M. & Bouffard, S. (2012) *Ready, Willing and Able*. Harvard Education Press
[84] RSA (2015) *The new digital learning age report*. RSA.org
[85] Freeman, K. (2004) *African Americans and College Choice. The Influence of Family and School*. SUNY Press

Skills Networks

Skills networks can play an important role in reaching harder to reach groups, particularly if they include organisations that help individuals develop skills awareness, confidence and self-determination. Skills networks can help deliver a public good to groups where socio-economic factors affect learning and life choices and trajectories.

An important role that skills networks can also play is to identify and map skills, including skills needs, skills gaps and skills that might be undervalued or hidden in the local context. Such information provides a source of data that could be drawn on and clustered to provide insights for organisational learning campaigns and skills conduits.

Additional Unseens

While skills visibility is one area that is often poorly seen but where we think organisations can release significant value, there are many areas that may be unseen or challenging to see with existing tools and processes. This lack of insight can affect an organisation's ability to maximise sales revenue and optimise operations.

These include things that affect sales such as a client's cultural and structural readiness to implement a new piece of technology or service, or more tangible unseens such as how global events might affect supply chains and ultimately stock control.

Unseens can also affect performance, such as the experiences or frustrations that impact remote workers, or processes that limit collaboration across teams, organisations or nations.

Gaining visibility and releasing the value of these unseens can be empowered by the cultural and structural behaviours of mesh organisations and enhanced through developments in Web3. We explore these in more depth in the chapter on Web3 solutions but next we will explore another significant area of operations that can benefit from increased visibility - contributions and deployment.

Optimising Deployment

14.
Contribution Visibility

Releasing Value

A lack of insight about contribution and where, what and how it is occurring, acts as an organisational circuit breaker affecting operational functionality and the ability to rapidly innovate, manage remote work and coordinate contributions.

In this chapter we will explore this area where there is often limited visibility but where we think organisations can release significant value. We will consider it from an individual, team and global perspective and discuss: contribution awareness; articulation; capacity and pathways; balancing contributions; open contribution; contribution clusters; and decentralised contributions.

Contribution Visibility

The individuals that contribute to an organisation are often referred to in different ways depending on context, such as industry, function, or community, and may be called a participant, actor, maintainer or other such name. In an organisational context, individuals might also be referred to as an employee, team member, staff or talent. For the purposes of this chapter, we will refer to them using the collective term contributors. Each contributor has strengths and preferences in how they engage, produce and generate value.

Contributions involve taking in information, processing it to make decisions, and creating an output. The contributor's preferences will mean they tend towards jobs that involve certain things, like problem-solving, decision-making, advising others, community building, innovating, and so on. When contribution tendencies and preferences are visible and understood by the organisation, it enables better decision-making about how to balance teams, build solutions, and regenerate. It supports:

- Awareness of readily available skillsets that can contribute to tasks across the organisation
- The rapid development of effective and sustainable outputs

- Happier, intrinsically motivated individuals who enjoy contributing
- Psychological safety
- Improved morale and productivity by individuals and teams
- Reduced turnover as contributors are more invested in their work and can see their impact to 'the bigger picture'
- Ability to identify patterns and the function of the whole organisation
- The substantiation of concerns and feedback for decision-making from stakeholders
- The ability to tag and recognise contribution so that it might be remunerated or recognised with some other type of 'currency'

Individual

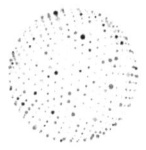

Contribution Awareness

An individual's understanding of their contribution tendencies will be informed by awareness of their decision-making preferences, skillsets and internal belief systems. Personal agency and self-directing abilities play a role in how an individual will contribute, while awareness of intrinsic motivators will lead them to focus on jobs that will help them thrive in the work environment.[86][87]

Motivation to contribute is affected by mindsets, leadership choices and context. For example, if a team is tasked with ideating, they are likely to be demotivated by an environment that does not support psychological safety. An individual's confidence in their capacity to perform tasks and achieve goals, their self efficacy, will also impact their motivation.[88] Confidence can be improved through a focus

---

[86] Maslow, A.H. (1954) *Motivation and personality.* Harpers
[87] Bandura, A. (1982) *Self-efficacy mechanism in human agency.* American psychologist, 37(2), 122
[88] Bandura, A. (2001) *Social Cognitive Theory and Clinical Psychology.* International Encyclopedia of Social & Behavioral Sciences. 2001, p. 14250-14254. Pergamon

on developing a mesh mindset and the individual receiving recognition for their skills and contribution.

Mesh organisations seek to recruit and retain individuals whose skills can be deployed across the organisation rather than just within fixed roles, and contribution awareness is important for achieving this goal.

Contribution Articulation

When contributions are articulated in a way that is understood and made visible, they can be effectively used. Understanding contribution tendencies aids deployment of the most appropriate contributor for the task.

There are many ways in which contribution tendencies might manifest so we will only consider a couple of generalised examples to explore this concept. Some individuals will enjoy and be competent at moving between the micro and the macro, whereas others will have a preference more for one than the other. For contributors who prefer working in the microcosm, this might manifest as contribution tendencies for: research, gathering detailed information or maintaining project outcomes. For those who prefer the macrocosm, this might manifest as contribution tendencies for: developing new concepts, pioneering new ideas, creating innovative solutions, forging new identities or creating ways forward during times of uncertainty.

Each contributor has a value to offer within the contexts of an organisation that can influence change, information processing and collaboration. Understanding of this contribution enables it to be directed and used in meaningful and productive ways.

Contribution Capacity & Pathways

The capacity for contribution is informed by an individual's motivation to contribute, their desire to regenerate and the organisation's capacity to enable and empower the contributor. Pathways to preferred types of contribution rely on the individual's actions to expand their capacity and to learn.

Continual learning is part of a mesh mindset, including using learning to adapt. Learning agility prompts development of the capacity for adapting to situations quickly and applying knowledge from prior experience to tackle new challenges in new contexts. Studies suggest an individual's learning agility can be a predictor of long-term performance and leadership potential.[89]

Mesh organisations support an individual expanding their contribution capacity by valuing and providing opportunities for learning and ensuring contributions are

---

[89] De Meuse, K. (2017) *Learning agility: Its evolution as a psychological construct and its empirical relationship to leader success.* Consulting Psychology Journal: Practice and Research

visible and recognised to develop better understanding of contribution tendencies and preferences.

Team

Balancing Contributions

In mesh organisations contributions of varying types are seen and valued. Visibility of skills and contributions means contribution clusters can be formed more easily, helping organisations to balance teams and optimise their power to generate value.

The rapid innovation of the open source technology sector demonstrates that balancing input from a mix of backgrounds, perspectives and skills can lead to more considered and robust products and services.[90] Balancing different contribution tendencies can aid team outputs, while balanced contributions in collaborative efforts aid sustainability. Each contributor can add a capability that can be used to balance efforts by how they make decisions, how

---

[90] Whitehurst, J. (2015) *The Open Organization: Igniting Passion and Performance.* Harvard Business Review Press

they respond to uncertainty, how they influence others around them and how they generate value.

Capabilities & Contributions Capacity

Organisational designs that result in people being treated like machines are outmoded. Technologically advanced but decentralised workplaces need to develop human-centricity if they wish to maximise their generative capabilities. As we have explored, individuals feel empowered when they can contribute with agency and in ways that align with their intrinsic motivations. Enabling individuals within teams to contribute in such ways, helps organisations realise the fullest extent of the value they can offer.

Mesh organisations aim to ensure that operational and organisational capacities enable optimal contributions with minimal resistance. In our work helping organisations to identify and release TUV, we have often found the blocks in capacity are due to redundant processes in workflows, silos preventing information flow, and lack of visibility across the organisation. These can create pockets of resistance rather than helping contribution flow to where it optimally needs to go.

Research examining employment-related motivations post the Covid-19 pandemic, identified the need for more human-centric work practices.[91] Technology coupled with cultural practices that promote connection, visibility and trust can help organisations create an environment for people to be more human, which in turn has the positive benefit of increasing the organisation's generative capacity.

Deployment

Strategies and processes commonly used in relation to deployment include talent acquisition, talent management, talent deployment and performance management. These strategies and processes influence how the individuals and skills in an organisation are recruited, deployed and remunerated. In recent decades, this work has often been considered the sole remit of a Human Resources department but with the capacities for connection and visibility created by mesh culture and structure, and with developments in Web3, it is possible to think beyond a single department in terms of how to use, deploy and remunerate contributions.

Mesh organisations identify the optimal contributors for a given task, consider how different types of contributions impact outcomes, and use contribution visibility to swiftly deploy individuals so they can contribute optimally. This requires knowing what roles or projects need filling, an individual's skills clusters, if that individual is

---

[91] Wiles, J. (2022) *Employees Seek Personal Value and Purpose at Work*. Gartner

available and willing to participate, and any considerations that will impact their contribution. For example, if the best individual identified is not employed within the organisation, the organisation might consider open contribution.

A mesh organisational design, paired with tools to aid connection and visibility of contribution, could have a significant impact on deployment.

Global

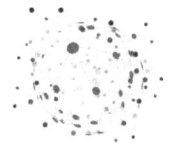

Open Contribution

Broadly speaking, open contribution makes it possible for contributors external to an organisation to contribute to it. Examples of open contribution can be found in the development of open source software or crowdsourcing for participation through voting, collaboration or completion of micro-tasks.

In our experience with open communities, we have witnessed firsthand how open collaboration can yield rapid innovation, connected people, intriguing ideas, and strong outcomes. Drawing on an example from the Open Organization, numerous books have been collectively written by this open knowledge community, each taking roughly six months to produce from topic ideation to publication. Book topics were determined by an Ambassador team, and after a call for chapters was issued, the community used an open source code repository to submit chapter topics and text, and used pull requests for suggestions and editing. Contributors of varying industry backgrounds from all over the world compiled experience, skills, insights and knowledge into the books.

In another example, the first version of the open recognition standard, Open Badges, was created by globally distributed contributors providing ideas and code via an open source code repository, collaborative documents and community calls facilitated by the Mozilla Foundation. This standard is used by organisations around the world, including by companies that regularly feature in lists of the top five most profitable companies globally, which serves to highlight how robust, useful and trusted outputs developed in a decentralised way can be.

In these scenarios, open collaboration was supported by documented processes and governance, open engagement with communities, digital tools and the contributors themselves. Within a decentralised world, success is aided by structures and technology that create capacity for visibility and contribution, and build trust through community engagement.

Contribution Clusters

In the Mesh Model chapter, we stated that conceptually we can think of mesh organisations as having power sources, a power plant and power brokers. Each of these have a (re)generative purpose and they contain components that can cluster and re-cluster to sustain and expand the organisation's reach.

The core power source is a cluster of contributors that form the leadership team and empower the operational functioning of the power plant. As a container and generative conductor, the power plant catalyses collective contributions. Within the mesh of the power plant are clusters of components, including individuals who call on different clusters of skills to perform various tasks, and who can be clustered based on contribution tendencies to form balanced teams. The outputs from the organisational contributors are then received, used and amplified by demographic clusters in the external ecosystem, the power brokers.

These clusters are interconnected and interdependent, and contribute to not only optimising outputs but to ensuring the sustainability of the organisation itself. The contribution clusters create a contribution mesh that releases value inside the organisation and beyond.

Empowering Decentralised Contribution

Global challenges prompt a need for collaboration across borders and large-scale problem-solving. With the use of technology to empower decentralised contributions, organisations can deploy contributions with greater ease.

This may look like cross-functional deployment, where a contributor or cluster of contributors are deployed wherever their expertise and perspectives can help deliver a better outcome. By empowering the flexibility to contribute outside of fixed roles, organisations can additionally aid career growth by helping individuals upgrade their skills and explore different types of contribution. With visibility of external contributors, open collaboration can operate on a larger scale.

Visibility of where, what and how contributors can be accessed and optimally deployed positively impacts organisational success and sustainability. The ability to see contribution means micro-tasks can be tagged, recognised and rewarded appropriately. This is aided by Web3 technologies that enable discovery, recognition and remuneration of contributions, such as through the use of blockchains, smart contracts and tokens.

For this reason, and the many others discussed previously, we think Web3 technologies combined with human-centric organisational approaches can help empower a connected decentralised world.

Managing The Mesh

15.

Primer Tools

Putting mesh concepts into practice

You might find the following selection of abridged tools useful for getting started with embedding mesh concepts in your organisation.

These tools can be used by individuals, teams and organisations to aid developing a mesh mindset, moving towards a mesh culture and structure, and for navigating change. In this section, we cover:

- Mesh Readiness
- Organisational Design Prompts
- RBBL for TUV
- PENCIL (to help individuals approach regeneration)
- Mesh Learning Approaches (to aid collaborative learning and network formation)
- PRIMED (to help organisations approach regeneration)

Mesh Readiness

When considering your organisational clusters and their readiness, use the following prompts for conversation.

Core | Power Source Clusters

- Do we know the skills that exist across our organisation that are available for deployment?
- Do we know what skills gaps exist?
- Do we know how people are contributing in our organisation, or externally in the ecosystem?
- Do we hire for specific roles or for skills?
- Do we tie skills to a role type or do we allow for deployment of skills across the organisation?
- Do we create multi-disciplinary teams?
- Do we have a common shared language we use with our stakeholders to help them align with the organisation?
- Do our leaders facilitate conversations that bring others along and foster community with intention?
- Do our leaders adopt a macro, system-wide view and integrate understanding into the organisation?
- Do we shape practices that empower equity?

- Do we use democratic thinking to ensure boundaries are held for ethical sharing of information and feedback gathering?

Operational | Power Plant Clusters

- Are our software solutions and other components granular and interoperable?
- Do we make our software development visible across the organisation?
- Can organisational components be reused, remixed and repurposed?
- Do we draw on data from both internal and external sources?
- Do our processes and governance enable continual, small iterations?
- Does our organisational design empower mesh mindsets (regenerative, enlightenment, contribution)?
- Are our teams dynamic and fluid allowing for cross-functional collaboration?
- Do we have clearly defined common languages?
- Do we consistently use and implement trust practices?
- Do we enable and cultivate information flow?

Global | Power Broker Clusters

- Do we draw on external data to aid in insights for our business decisions?
- Are we aware of how our organisation is perceived?
- Do we foster meaningful external engagement with communities and customers?
- Do we have partnerships and support ecosystems?
- Do we collaborate openly internally and externally?
- Can we scale for decentralised activities and democratic decision-making?
- Do we provide clear, defined boundaries for the practice of ethical sharing of information, and enable user-control?

Organisational Design Prompts

For exploring culture and structures, use the following questions to generate productive conversations.
- Where are we today?
- Who are we today?
- What is our voice saying?
- What are we known for?
- How are we doing things?
- Why are we doing those things?

For exploring culture and structures for future state assessments, use the following questions to generate productive conversations.
- Where do we want to go?
- Who do we want to be?
- What do we want our voice to say?
- What do we want to be known for?
- How do we want to operate?
- Why will we do it this way?

When reviewing desired change and implementation goals, consider decisions through the core lens.

Ask: **"How will this change impact our people and/or leadership**," and fill in that blank with each of these terms:

- How does this impact our teams and departments?
- How does this reflect on competencies and skills development?
- How does this alter learning opportunities?
- How does this help or hinder contribution?
- How will we need to communicate now?

When reviewing desired change and implementation goals, consider decisions through the operational lens.

Ask: **"How will this change impact our processes or structures?,"** and fill in that blank with each of these terms:

- How does this change our way of operating and working?
- How does this affect our governance?
- Is information open and accessible?
- Does this affect our way of being?
- Are we balanced in our approach?
- Do we have the capacity to enable this change?
- What skills do we need to learn or use from our existing community to make this happen?

When reviewing desired change and implementation goals, consider decisions through the global lens.

Ask: **"How will this change impact our communities or wider set of connections?,"** and fill in that blank with each of these terms:

- How does this affect our internal stakeholders?
- How does this affect our external stakeholders?
- How does this impact our communities and partners?
- Does it affect our global impact or sustainability efforts?

After conducting collaborative sessions to discuss current and future states, and creating roadmaps for each stage, it is prudent to check against the mesh tenets. Over time, this becomes second nature as part of a continual state of evolution.

Mesh Mindsets

- Are we creating the capacity for adaptability?
- Do we provide space for experimentation and discovery?
- Do we provide learning opportunities for everyone?
- Do we encourage the development of awareness?
- Do we aid the articulation of skills, intrinsic motivators and contribution tendencies?
- Are we integrating insights from the wider system into the organisation?
- Are we willing to deconstruct what we know in order to regenerate and evolve?

Connection

- Are we connecting contributors and other organisational components?
- Are we collaborative in our approaches?
- Are we building communities with intention and to recognise contributions?
- Are we aligning our stakeholders with shared language and negotiating on clear outcomes?
- Are we considering the needs for expanded collaboration efforts?
- Are we assembling multi-disciplinary teams?

Visibility

- Are we identifying TUV and ways to release value?
- Are we making information, skills and contribution tendencies visible?
- Are we sharing materials for others to see and potentially contribute to?
- Are we exploring data and information to identify patterns to form connections?
- Are we able to articulate where we are in the change cycle? (See PENCIL)
- Are we drawing on the expertise and knowledge of stakeholders when making decisions?

Trust

- Are we empowering personal agency?
- Are we creating a psychologically safe environment and enabling all voices to be heard?
- Are we acting upon lessons learned?
- Are we encouraging individuals and communities to explore possibilities?
- Are we seeking consent to ensure boundaries and ethical practices when sharing information?
- Are we articulating clear goals and boundaries for scope of work and decision-making processes?

- Are we creating communities that provide value for its members?

RBBL for TUV

A Process for Gaining Awareness of Perceptions and Identifying Barriers & Limitations to Release TUV

Removing Bias, Barriers & Limitations (RBBL) for TUV is aligned with the five horizons of change as described in PENCIL. It can be executed as a thought exercise or used with mapping or flowchart tools.

Our lived experience provides context, definition and perspectives for each interaction we have. Data from external sources is processed as we interact with others, the media, and the world at large.

As we discussed in mesh mindsets, unconscious processing is informed by experiences, beliefs and conditioning, which if unchecked, can create limitations in thinking, behaviours and decision-making leading to personal TUV.

By investigating our thinking, we can identify what blocks us from engaging with certain situations, tasks, projects, or groups of people. Asking ourselves 'why?' aids discovery about our perceptions and can help us to remove limitations. This helps us grow and can help us connect and collaborate more effectively.

The first step is to identify current thinking related to the area under review, for example, a challenge that is being experienced. The investigation could include things like:
- Definitions of words being used
- Consideration of how our awareness might be limited
- Preconceptions and assumptions
- Feelings
- Past experiences
- Rules, standards, beliefs or even fears
- What we have heard from others
- Perspectives

After identifying any or all of these, begin to investigate the why, continuing this investigation until a root cause is discovered. Here are 'why?' prompts to assist this step:
- Why do I/we believe this?
- Why is this my/our context or belief?
- Why is this my/our understanding of this _____?
- Why do I/we feel this to be true?
- Why does my/our experience affect my understanding or decision making?
- Why does this process create a limitation of _____?

Before moving forward to the next stage, take a moment to reflect on the discovery. It is a critical point to recognise the limitations and blocks leading to TUV as they have the potential to impact numerous areas. The identification might lead to awareness of wider limiting behaviours in the organisation, the need to re-engineer workflows, or might bring enlightenment about a previously untapped revenue source.

The final steps of this exercise are to expand awareness, create actionable steps and allow for integration of the new flow of value. To do this we recommend creating statements that clearly define the problem and what the release of value will do.

Here are examples to guide the process.

Step 1: Be clear on the discovery so there is no confusion when sharing this information.

The issue creating trapped or untapped value is _____.

Step 2: Be clear on the symptoms of the trapped or untapped value being listed. This might be a list of symptoms you have uncovered.

This issue creates a limitation for me/us because _____.

Step 3: Craft a statement that shifts understanding and creates an actionable step for others. It may be written as a 'where we want to be' statement if helpful. This is a critical part of cognitive behavioural change even when referring to a workflow change.

We are now _____.

When this thinking tool is used regularly it helps develop awareness and TUV is continually identified so that value can be released.

PENCIL

A method we use to develop comfort with regeneration and change from an individual perspective is called PENCIL.

Navigating Change & Regenerating

Technology and digital transformation have been seen as the drivers of change for a number of years but they are only the products of change. Change starts with people. It is a personal experience and is engaged with contextually. How we interact with the change inherent in regeneration is based on our unique experiences and beliefs.

People have varying degrees of (dis)comfort when engaging with change and uncertainty. We can understand uncertainty as new information that we process while awaiting additional information. It is often considered an uncomfortable state to be in, both mentally and emotionally, as it challenges our current perception of reality and expectations about outcomes.

By gaining awareness of how we engage with change, we can increase our comfort with it. This starts by appreciating that we live in a continuous state of change by simply interacting with our environment. We enact changes as we adopt new information, process it and act accordingly.

It is worth noting here that not every change is positive. Sometimes resistance to change is due to limiting beliefs but sometimes it is because we think the change is unethical, harmful or will result in some other negative consequence. See the RBBL for TUV exercise to gain awareness about perceptions.

Change Horizons

We think of regeneration as a cyclical rather than linear process, which contains horizons that require an exchange to move from one to the next. Regeneration involves learning from what went before and to consciously dismantle and add to knowledge, to integrate learning in new contexts, and to loop around to start the process again.

We consider five horizons within the process of change. Personal capacity to effectively navigate each horizon commences with the first horizon of preparation.

Suggested thought prompts have been provided for each horizon.

Prepare

This horizon prompts us to prepare for the cycle and journey of change.

- Where am I today?
- Who am I today?
- Where am I going?
- Who do I want to be after this cycle of change?
- Who needs to come along on the journey with me?

Engage

This horizon requires a conscious choice to engage with what is new - such as information, people or technology.

- Am I ready to do this?
- Do I trust my ability to contribute and engage?
- Am I clear on what my colleagues and I are working towards?
- Do I need to develop a skill or learn a new one to contribute effectively?

Navigate

During the navigation horizon, we use approaches to create value, increase communal engagement, spur expansion, and foster trust.

- Are my behaviours fostering engagement and trust with others?
- Are my skills and contributions adding value?
- How can I adapt my skills and contributions to add value?
- What am I learning from this to take into the next horizon?
- What TUV am I discovering?

Course correct

During the horizon of course correction, we observe, adjust, iterate and refine to continue towards our preferred outcome.

- What is working or not working at this time?
- With the information gathered in the previous horizon, what adjustments need to be made?
- What limitations or barriers can I remove?
- What TUV can be released now?

Integrate

At the horizon of integration we have adopted the change.
- Is this new way of doing things part of my daily routine?
- Is my mindset creating minimal resistance to the change?
- Does the change feel natural and is it easy to socialise?

Loop

The final horizon in the change cycle begins with a loop round to the next cycle where we begin to discover and prepare for the next regeneration.

Mesh Learning Approach

The Mesh Learning Approach is an approach to learning that aids the process of individual, team and organisational regeneration and helps individuals develop behaviours and practices that aid the functioning of a mesh organisation.

It can be used to rapidly integrate new knowledge as an individual, within teams and throughout the organisation. It draws on the tenets of connection, visibility and trust and provides a compass for collaborative learning experiences.

The Mesh Learning Approach:

1. Acknowledges the regenerative nature of learning and the change horizons an individual crosses as they deconstruct and reconstruct meaning and cycle between the different perspectives of inner understanding and external context.

2. Supports connection, visibility and trust by: connecting new concepts to participants' own contexts to yield personalised outcomes; peers sharing practice; and the provision of a psychologically safe learning environment.

3. Are open learning experiences that draw on the principles of open education and open recognition.

4. Focus on practices that activate and foster sustainable cycles of learning.

Horizons

Learning is active, never passive. It involves consciously making a choice to accept the challenge of dismantling and adding to existing knowledge, and applying that learning in new contexts.

The change cycle inherent to learning involves crossing horizons of understanding and opening up new realms of awareness. Ambiguity and chaos exists in the process of deconstructing knowledge and reconstructing to form new meaning. This transformation can be difficult because it involves challenging pre-existing notions and understanding. The challenge associated with learning is likely to account for the ceremonies that accompany learning, such as award ceremonies, in recognition of what has been achieved.

Providing adequate space for learning is important. The process of learning benefits from preparation mentally and emotionally for the change that will be experienced - there will be a transformation, from which the learner will emerge with new understanding.

Regeneration

The capacity for lifelong learning is regulated by the individual.[92] Change commences from the self and understanding of internal behaviours and attitudes means they can be appropriately applied, challenged or changed to optimise contribution. Prompting individuals to engage in continual cycles of learning about their own behaviours and attitudes, helps them develop self-awareness and become self-directing learners, adapting and regenerating to contribute at their best and gain the most from their careers. (See RBBL for TUV)

Liminality

Learning involves a metaphorical journey, traversing liminal spaces and crossing horizons of understanding. A liminal space is a transitional space that occupies one or both sides of a threshold or horizon. When learning, individuals traverse liminal spaces as they engage with the process of deconstructing and reconstructing meaning, and cycling between these states.

We reference the Change Horizons from PENCIL for the horizons of a learning journey.

---

[92] Nicol, D. (2021) *The power of internal feedback: exploiting natural comparison processes.* Assessment and Evaluation in Higher Education, 46(5), pp. 756-778

Preparing & Engaging

Before starting on a specific course of learning, individuals make a choice, consciously or not, to metaphorically start a learning journey. At the start of that learning journey they will be unclear exactly where it will go, what new insights they will gather along the way and where they will end up. They may have a goal they are moving towards but how the process of learning will affect them, is unknown until they are on the journey.

Motivation

The knowledge that a learning experience will involve a journey involving cycles of destruction, reconstruction, and unforeseen challenges, compels the setting aside of mental and emotional resources. Being clear on motivations can help individuals to cross hurdles as they encounter them and stay the course.[93] Intrinsic motivation, where something is undertaken because of inherent enjoyment, can provide individuals with additional resources for meeting the challenges they will encounter along the way.[94]

---

[93] Deci, E. & Ryan, R. (2000) *Intrinsic and Extrinsic Motivations: Classic Definitions and New Directions.* Contemporary Educational Psychology 25,54–67 (2000)
[94] Deci, E. & Ryan, R. (2010) *Intrinsic Motivation.* The Corsini Encyclopedia of Psychology

Navigation & Course Correction

Collaborative Learning

Collaborative learning experiences have a positive impact on the effective functioning of a mesh organisation as they help individuals develop behaviours that support connection, visibility and trust.

Individuals elevate their learning when they learn socially, constructing knowledge and meaning through discussion and collaboration.[95] The experience of learning with peers, sharing practice and co-creating, fosters network creation and collaboration.[96]

Team learning experiences become highly generative when they are collaborative.[97] Within the group, each individual will have expertise in their area of influence, which the facilitator endeavours to draw out. The knowledge in the room creates a richer, more contextualised learning experience from which everyone can gain new insights and understanding.

Individuals are invited to share their contexts and perspectives, and content and discussion is adapted based

---

[95] Vygotsky, L. S. (1978) *Mind in society: the development of higher psychological processes.* London: Harvard University Press
[96] Piaget, J. (1936) *Origins of intelligence in the child.* London: Routledge & Kegan Paul
[97] Hamilton, G. & Blair, J. (2005) *Online Collaborative Learning in Social Work Education.* Ardcairn Publications

on this. Weaving presentation of theory around group conversation, and responding to questions and considerations as they arise, results in deeper learning. Balancing presentation of theory and new concepts, with exploration of learners' own contexts and encouragement to share practice amongst peers, yields personalised outcomes.

Participants learn from other participants as well as from those leading the learning experience. The sharing of practice and links to resources is encouraged to create an immersive, peer-powered learning experience.

Connection

Communities form through a sense of connection and common interests. A sense of community can help an individual feel they belong and provide a psychological safety net that helps them explore, fail, iterate, and engage fully with the learning process. Learning communities can be initiated by inviting participants to share some aspects of themselves and their lives to help individuals identify common points of interest and to remind each other of joint humanity. Feelings of connection help to build trust and help individuals be more open to sharing, which helps yield the richest learning experience as participants share openly and contribute to the learning of the group.

Individuals learn through their connections and by making connections, tapping into networks, accessing resources, and connecting ideas.[98] Knowing where to find information can be just as important as what an individual knows, and by learning with peers, individuals can share and discover resources pertinent to their own contexts.

Visibility

The active process of learning compels learners to deconstruct their existing knowledge and reconstruct it with new insights to forge new meaning. This process can be difficult and leave learners feeling vulnerable as they traverse liminal spaces. In mesh learning experiences, there are no right or wrong questions, it is a safe space to explore concepts and be transparent about the challenges of the learning process, to question, explore, reflect, fail, try again and iterate to develop new understandings.

Individuals broaden their perspectives by asking questions but also learn vicariously by hearing the questions asked by peers and understanding the issues that concern them.[99] This peer-generated material yields insights for individuals and the team, and provides understanding about the wider organisation.

---

[98] Siemens, G. (2004) *Connectivism: A Learning Theory for the Digital Age.* elearnspace
[99] Mayes, T. (1997) *Dialogue with a Dumb Terminal.* The Times Education Supplement

Trust

Individuals are empowered when they are in an environment they trust. The process of learning is naturally quite messy and chaotic, which can lead to feelings of vulnerability. It involves making mistakes, cycling through hypotheses, comparing and contrasting, iterating ideas and questioning oneself. Feeling safe to engage is essential and knowing that failing is allowed and celebrated as part of the learning process, is vital. Feeling psychologically safe and able to communicate in a style that works best for them, helps put individuals at ease and feel empowered to engage.[100]

Learning experiences that cater for diverse perspectives, communication styles and neurodiversity help everyone to learn. Providing multiple ways to participate and contribute, and encouraging participants to make themselves comfortable, helps enable this.

---

[100] Edmondson, A. (1999) *Psychological Safety and Learning Behavior in Work Teams*. Sage Publications

Open

Open learning

Open learning empowers learners to learn at their own time, at their own pace and in a variety of ways. It provides access to granular learning assets and opportunities that can be remixed and repurposed by individuals to create flexible and personalised learning pathways.

Open Recognition

Open recognition empowers learner-controlled and flexible recognition of learning and skills via granular, shareable, verifiable and interoperable digital credentials.[101] These provide useful insights, which can help the individual make better informed decisions about learning and career pathways based on intrinsic motivation.

Recognition of the wide range of skills an individual has, not just those required for a fixed role, is also highly valuable to the organisation by providing nuanced information about the competencies and attributes available for it to draw on, empowering enhanced skill based recruitment, deployment and team formation.

---

[101] The Mozilla Foundation et al. (2010) *Open Badges for Lifelong Learning.* Mozilla Foundation

Integration & Loop

Sustainable Transformation

The final part of a learning cycle is integration of the learning in new contexts. Sustainable transformation involves a continual cycle of learning and application, shifting between different realms of awareness, and mapping and weaving new insights into understanding. The whole process starts again, as the individual finds new information to learn from and engages in new learning opportunities. As individuals increase knowledge of themselves, what motivates them, and how their behaviours impact their external experience, they refine their ability to develop sustainably and generate better outcomes for themselves and the organisation.

PRIMED

Thrive today and prime for tomorrow.

A method we use to aid the continual process of organisational regeneration is called PRIMED. It provides quick prompts for considering types of tools and processes that could be used for discovering TUV, gaining visibility, integrating changes, evaluating if value has been released and what improvements could be made next. The prompts are not intended as an exhaustive list but to inspire ideas.

Prepare

In this stage, the organisation seeks to identify what improvements could be made. This might be through the use of:

- Diagnostics
- Researching and identifying new tools
- Researching and identifying new data sources

Run

This stage involves applying the insights gathered from the preparation stage. This might be through:

- Forming and implementing plans based on the outcomes of diagnostics
- Testing new tools
- Clustering different data sources

Integrate

In this stage, there is integration of the work done in the previous stages. This might include:
- Integrating lessons learned from the implementation of new practices or processes
- Scaling up the use of new tools
- Making more nuanced use of new data sources

Manoeuvre

Regeneration is a continual cycle of tweaks and iterations. When new practices or processes have been integrated into an organisation it is not the end of the journey. In this stage, we would expect to see:
- Re-diagnosis to identify progress
- Identification of nuanced reasons for issues
- Course correction

Evaluate

This stage involves panning out to evaluate the wider impact on the organisation and culture. This could be through:
- Diagnostics
- Surveys
- Focus Groups

Discover

At this point the process starts again, looping around to discover new areas of TUV, and to implement new iterative improvements.

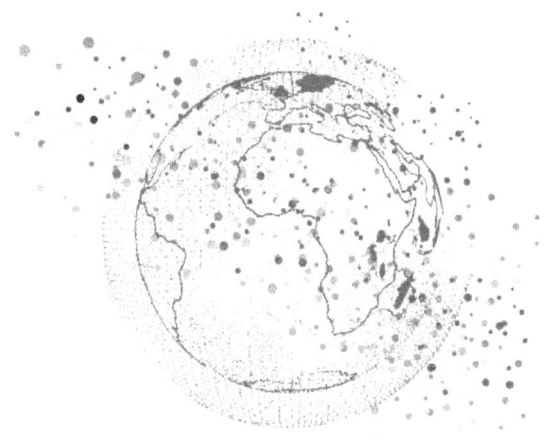

Emergence

16.
Web3 Solutions

The challenges that organisations face exist within a context of emerging technology that we think could aid their response to the challenges. Web3, powered by smart contracts, blockchains, AI and tokenization provide numerous opportunities for organisations to gain better insights, enhance connection, and generate trust for organisational benefit.

Optimising for Web3

Mesh culture and structures influence, and are influenced by, granular, flexible components that can be clustered, reused, remixed and repurposed. Optimal technology solutions for mesh organisations, therefore, will be defined by and capitalise on the principles of granularity and flexibility.

The nature of Web3 caters for this and provides opportunities for novel solutions such as using AI to collate and cluster data from multiple, distributed data sources to generate meaningful insights, or managing remote contribution with smart contracts and tokenization.

The following examples outline just a few of the scenarios that could be aided by Web3 technologies. In each we have added a trust note. While Web3 provides more opportunities for users to control their data, any consideration of collecting and using data, requires careful consideration of ethics and an individual's right to privacy.

Sales Insights

One of the key points of concern for many organisations is sales. Web3 technologies enable organisations to draw on multiple, distributed data sources, and collate and cluster that data with AI, to generate visual dashboards that can be filtered for various functions and departments.

Such data might relate to things that affect sales. For example, a technology company may wish to ascertain a client's cultural and structural readiness to implement open source technology. Insights might be generated via internal data gathered from questions gathered on calls and complemented with external data sources such as research relating to open source maintenance and sustainability. These insights could be gathered, collated, filtered, clustered and presented to provide insights to account managers, sales personnel, the marketing department and senior management to influence how the organisation markets and sells its products.

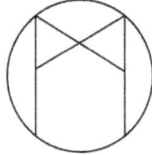

Trust Note: Ensuring consent is vital for trust, such as by drawing on user-controlled data or ensuring data use has been opted into or consented to at source.

Anti-Trust: Failure to seek consent or respect user choice regarding their data will lead to an erosion of trust.

Skills Discovery and Deployment

Having a skills map of an organisation, rather than a purely role-based organisational chart, generates opportunities for beneficial insights to optimise recruitment, retention and deployment.

Drawing on skills data from a variety of sources, and being able to collate, interrogate and cluster these, will yield a more nuanced picture of an individual's and the organisation's skills and capabilities than can be ascertained from role titles alone.

Multi-source skills dashboards help individuals gain awareness of their skills and skill gaps, helping them to become lifelong, self-regulating learners. For organisational leaders, such dashboards help identify the skills present in the organisation, which can be used to deploy skills to projects, address skills gaps and aid planning for future skills needs.

A more granular approach to skills recognition globally would complement this internal organisational data and enable the organisation to discover skills and draw on them accordingly. Open recognition can also be used to develop skills conduits and initiatives to support more equitable access to learning opportunities and skills recognition for harder to reach groups.[102]

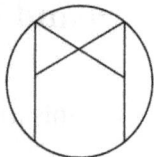

Trust Note: Acknowledging the person and that the skills exist and can be developed because they are generated by an individual (human-centricity) is essential for trust. Ensuring consent is also vital for trust, such as by drawing on user-controlled data or ensuring data use has been opted into or consented to at source.

Anti-Trust: Dehumanising the person by seeing them only as a cluster of skills, and using personal data without their consent will lead to an erosion of trust, lack of motivation and lack of psychological safety.

---

[102] Painter, A., and Shafique, A. (2017) *Cities of Learning in the UK Prospectus.* RSA.

Remote Work Management

Remote work creates a number of opportunities and challenges for organisations. It provides flexibility and can help individuals fit work in around other life commitments, thereby positively impacting their lifestyle. This flexibility can also help organisations tap into valuable skills that otherwise might be closed off to them as a result of geography or capacity, such as parents juggling child-minding and work commitments.

One of the aspects of remote work that frustrates some organisations, however, is the lack of ability to see what a colleague is doing. They cannot walk through to the next office to see what is happening. Conversely, an aspect of remote work that frustrates individuals is if they think they are being tracked for every micro-action because they are not trusted to do their job.

This is where the tenets of mesh organisations become important and the condition of balance is vital. The cultural behaviours of mesh organisations prompt leaders to balance visibility with trust. If individuals think they are being tracked from a punitive perspective, they will feel they are not trusted and their sense of personal agency will be undermined. These feelings can produce a significant negative impact for the organisation, cause TUV and inhibit generative performance.

Moving the metric and methods for rewarding contribution in this context could help remove or reduce these blocks and rebuild trust and performance. Using smart contracts to release value, such as to show task completion progress or to release money or some other form of currency upon completion of specified tasks, moves the onus for tracking input from punitive to valuable. Value isn't rewarded based on the number of hours spent on a job but on tasks being completed. Reward is released at the pace at which the individual wishes or is able to work and provides a motivation to maintain a pace of work that would also reflect the organisation's needs.

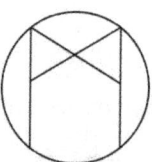

Trust Note: Acknowledging the person and ensuring completion times for task smart contracts are agreed based on the individual's capacity (human-centricity) will help maintain trust. If the individual can complete the same tasks in half a day that in a non-contract setting would normally take a full day, it is a testament to their effort and self-organising capacities. The reason they are more productive may be because they are working remotely without office-related distractions and have the flexibility to focus and concentrate their effort into a shorter period of time. The same effort is still required to complete the tasks whether they deliver in half a day or a day.

Anti-Trust: Setting exhausting or continuously increasing targets for tasks to be completed is likely to lead to demotivation, which will inhibit generation and potentially cause burnout, resulting in additional costs for recruiting and onboarding new people.

Collaboration Across Borders

Collaboration across teams, organisations and nations has been empowered with the ubiquitous communication facilities of Web2. Collaborative events can be engaged in without hours of travel, from the participants' locations, with collaboration tools to aid mind-mapping, instant messaging and video conferencing.

This proliferation of tools, and the distributed developments of collaborative initiatives, however, can pose challenges. There is a chance of developments becoming siloed if there isn't a conscious effort to connect them.

Standards can provide a framework for enabling interoperability, discovery and connection between distributed developments but Web3 enabled visualisation and connection dashboards would also be beneficial. The ability to collate data from different tools being used, and from the distributed developments, would provide insights to those facilitating and participating in the collaboration to keep developments on track.

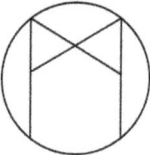

Trust Note: Ensuring consent is vital for trust, such as by drawing on user-controlled data or ensuring data use has been opted into or consented to at source.

Anti-Trust: Failure to seek consent or respect user choice regarding their data will lead to an erosion of trust.

17.
Emergence & Expansion

Mesh

Mesh is a human-centric organisational design that helps generate connection, visibility and trust. It is informed by a conceptual model built upon the principles and structures of meshes, nodes, orbs, clusters and power generation and is formed of:

An *open and regenerative culture* and leadership that catalyses the components and connections in the organisation to get the most value out of every part, and promotes organisational behaviours that can optimise the benefits of decentralisation;

A *mesh structure* formed of granular and potentially distributed components that can connect, interact, generate value and draw others into their orbit, and that capitalise on the value that can be derived from reusing, remixing and repurposing flexible internal and external components such as evolving data sets, and the intellectual capital of cross-organisational and external communities;

Web3 solutions such as blockchain, tokenization, and smart contracts to manage the mesh, and visualisation tools to enable collating, connecting and clustering of data from a variety of sources to provide helpful insights, to optimise processes, and to release value.

These elements are enmeshed - the structure informs the culture, the culture informs the structure, and both create a generative environment primed for Web3.

An Economic Challenge

As we have considered throughout this book, regeneration creates opportunities and challenges. By capitalising on the opportunities provided by decentralisation and Web3, the Mesh organisational design enables scenarios such as contribution outside of fixed roles or employment, and micro-tasks managed with smart contracts. These developments enable individuals to seek tasks that align with their skills and intrinsic motivations so they can contribute at their best.

However, if we consider the consequences of wide-scale adoption of such scenarios, they present an economic challenge that has long been highlighted in relation to the 'gig economy'[103] - how to ensure individuals can meet their basic income, and other needs, if they are not

---

[103] Malik, R., et al. (2021) *The Gig Economy: Current Issues, the Debate, and the New Avenues of Research.* Sustainability 13, no. 9. MDPI

employed full-time in a salaried role. How the new opportunities and challenges related to decentralisation will affect the next generation of money design and economics is being explored but it is an area where more research is vital if trust is to be built for wide-scale application of this way of working.

Human-Centricity in a Decentralised World

In an increasingly digital and decentralised world, human-centric approaches are vital. The Mesh organisational design empowers individuals to flourish within a culture and structure that generates connection, visibility and trust, and helps organisations to power performance, see the unseen and optimise deployment. Drawing on principles to be found in nature and the regenerative power of people, Mesh enables organisations to manage decentralisation, release value and capitalise on Web3 - to thrive today and navigate tomorrow.

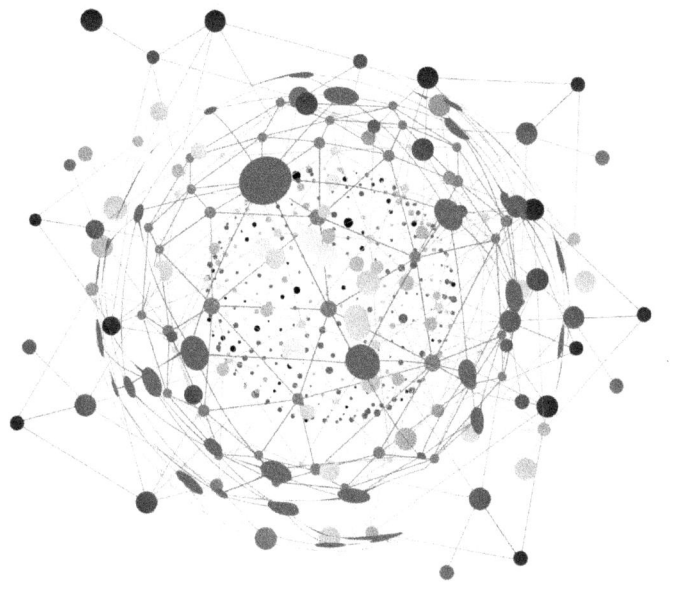

Acknowledgements

We have been influenced by many wonderful people over the course of our work, who have helped us form the organisational design that we describe in this book. To our families, and the friends we made along the way, thank you for your support - we are grateful to you.

We would like to mention a few people who have had a particular input to the creation of this book. Thank you to Bryan D. Eldridge for your keen insights on Web3 that helped us expand our concept. Your ability to simplify the more complex nuances of emerging technology to align with our vision has been invaluable to us.

Thank you also to Robert McIntyre for your insights on James Clerk Maxwell, on engineering concepts more broadly, on the features of high-reliability organisations, and for your willingness to act as an industry sounding board for our ideas. In addition, we are grateful to Bryan Behrenshausen for helping us expand our understanding of open source sustainability and, alongside Douglas Ferguson and Robert Thorne, for providing valuable production insights for this book.

There are many others we could thank, too many to mention here but we are grateful to those who have generously shared their ideas and time and joined us on our journey.

Glossary

Agile approaches: describes an approach where ideas are explored, co-created and tested in rapid cycles, enabling teams to learn fast and develop resilient solutions.

Artificial Intelligence (AI): can be thought of as machine generated intelligence or learning that helps the machine to refine how it makes decisions or presents information to a user.

Blockchains: enable transactions to be managed collectively by a network rather than by a controlling authority. They are ledgers of facts and transactions that provide immutable records through cryptography.

Clusters: groups of items. Can be broken apart and re-clustered and like fractals, clusters can exist within clusters. Enable patterns to be found and insights revealed. Can be applied to things such as individuals, teams, skills and contributions.

COG: acronym for Core, Operational and Global. Lenses that aid consideration of different parts of an organisation.

Conditions: conditions that aid implementation of the Mesh organisational design. Additionally, they catalyse the culture and provide guiding principles for the structure of a mesh organisation.

Conditions, ORBITALS: Open; Regeneration; Balance; Information flow; Trust practices; Awareness; Learning; and Sustainability

Contribution deployment: can be thought of as talent deployment or talent management strategy; managing an organisation's employees' contributions.

Contribution tendency: can be thought of as the decision-making preferences, skillsets and internal belief systems that inform ways an individual tends to contribute and may manifest itself in areas such as problem-solving, decision-making, advising others, community building, innovating, and so on.

Cryptocurrencies: use blockchain technology to manage financial transactions.

Data Mesh Architecture: draws on and enables management of distributed data from multiple sources rather than from a restricted set of data available within a monolithic database.

Decentralisation: can be thought of as activities, decision-making processes and components that are distributed, potentially away from the control of an organisation.

Fixed processes: can be considered as processes that do not allow for much flexibility, such as rigidly defined roles which individuals are not expected to, or will be reprimanded for, acting outside of.

Lens, Core: the leadership team; also an individual's self-awareness and conscious and unconscious behaviours. (Orb) The *power source*.

Lens, Global: Wider context and engagement. (Orbiting ecosystem) The *power broker*.

Lens, Operational: Organisational processes and frameworks. (Mesh) The *power plant*.

Lenses: can be used to consider the structure of an organisation and gain a rounded perspective of it.

Gig economy: denotes work delivered and undertaken via short-term contracts by individuals who are not employed or in a fully-salaried role and who select 'gig' contracts through online platforms.

Mesh: a structure made up of a network of nodes. A conceptual element used to describe features of the mesh model. The name of a human-centric organisational design that helps organisations generate connection, visibility and trust to power performance, see the unseen and optimise deployment to release value, manage decentralisation and prime for Web3.

Mesh Learning Approach: an approach to learning that aids the process of individual, team and organisational regeneration and helps individuals develop behaviours and practices that aid the functioning of a mesh organisation.

Mesh Method: an approach for implementing the Mesh organisational design that employs the lenses of COG; is formed around the tenets of: Connection, Visibility and Trust; and applies the conditions of ORBITALS:

Mesh Model: a visual blueprint that supports system thinking by drawing on metaphors to illustrate the key features and principles of the Mesh organisational design.

Mesh Network: enables a number of distributed points to connect and communicate with each other to dynamically route data efficiently over as wide an area as possible.

Mesh Organisation: organisations that use the principles and structure of a mesh model to maximise value from the various components that contribute to it. These components may be distributed internally or externally, and include individuals, data and technology.

Mesh processes: can be considered as processes that are the opposite of fixed processes and that allow for flexibility, such as the ability to work outside of defined roles.

Mindset, Contribution: understand how an individual prefers to contribute to assign them to work that plays to their strengths

Mindset, Enlightenment: prompts an individual or leader to push beyond current understanding that may be limiting their capacity or creating limitations, barriers or bias.

Mindset, Learning: helps individuals to regenerate and adapt to changing circumstances; Continual learning, including learning about what worked and what didn't, helps individuals to increase their awareness about their own patterns of behaviour and how this impacts those around them

Mindset, Mesh: include regenerative, enlightenment and contribution mindsets

Mindset, Regenerative: how individuals and leaders engage with change through the process of developing awareness, the action of learning and integrating new understanding

Mindset: how individuals think, feel, act and process information and change.

Nodes: a point through which one or more connections meet. In the Mesh organisational design, nodes provide a way of conceptualising components that can be connected to the rest of the mesh structure and through which information can flow. In an organisational context nodes can be individuals, teams or technology

Open approaches: The following provides insights into some of the most popular open approaches: Open data can be accessed from the original creator and repurposed and reused in new contexts while open licensing makes clear how content can be reused and if it can be repurposed.[104] Open education removes traditional barriers to entry such as the requirement for pre-existing qualifications in order to participate,[105] while open educational resources (OERs) package learning in bite-sized chunks that can be collated and remixed for different educational purposes.[106] With open recognition, qualifications and other forms of recognition of skills are not siloed within formal education institutions or single systems but take the form of granular, digital credentials created to an open standard. This enables skills to be recognised by anyone, shared across the web by the recipient, and clustered for different purposes.[107] Open components such as these can be contributed to, drawn on, re-packaged and repurposed to be made available for a wider community or for organisation-specific uses. Irrespective of whether they are engaged with as part of an external community or only within and across an organisation, these types of components compel people to work and contribute in open ways. Data and participation is open for others to see, share, scrutinize, comment on, reuse, remix and repurpose. This exposure to others' input and the

---

[104] Creative Commons
[105] Wiley, D. (2007) *The MOOC Guide*. The Wiley Wiki
[106] Littlejohn, A. and Hood, N. (2017), *How educators build knowledge and expand their practice: The case of open education resources*. Br J Educ Technol, 48: 499-510
[107] Open Badges

decentralised control of some of these approaches requires behaviours and a culture that empowers openness and regenerative behaviours.

Open characteristics: The global knowledge community, the Open Organization, has considered core characteristics of organisations that routinely use and benefit from open source technology. These characteristics provide a useful starting point for considering cultural norms and behaviours that help teams maximise the opportunities provided by being able to make changes to open source code.[108] They are: *adaptability, collaboration, community, transparency* and *inclusivity*.

Open contribution: broadly speaking it makes it possible for contributors external to an organisation to contribute to it.

Open source software: software with code that is made openly available so others can adapt and contribute to it. It enables contextualisation for an individual organisation's or team's needs and open contributors can help develop a piece of software used by others. Open source solutions are considered particularly robust and secure with many perspectives and skills contributing to the problems of developing it.

---

[108] The Open Organization Ambassadors. (2017) *The Open Organization Definition*. OpenSource.com

ORBITALS: acronym for Open, Regeneration, Balance, Information flow, Trust practices, Awareness, Learning, Sustainability

Orb: a spherical shape that allows rapid connection across and to every part of the structure. A conceptual element used to describe features of the mesh model.

Organisational design: a methodology to identify aspects of workflow, processes, governance, structures and systems to allow for goals to be met and change implemented; includes both people and technical aspects of an organisation

Organisational culture: the values and behaviours that contribute to the unique social and psychological environment of an organisation. For us it is the ethos, values, and frameworks for how a company conducts itself internally and externally. Culture includes core values, expectations for behaviour, decision-making frameworks, how information flows through the organisation, and how it conducts itself with others.

Organisational structure: how an organisation is architected. It includes governance, processes, systems and workflows, and how these can be aligned or realigned for business goals. Structure influences information flow and how organisations behave through the coordination of tasks and decision-making to meet their goals.

PENCIL: The acronym for the change horizons of a method that can be used to develop comfort with regeneration and change from an individual perspective: Prepare; Engage; Navigate; Course-correct; Integrate; and Loop.

Personal agency: having a sense of agency and ownership of one's work, and a belief that "I am the cause of my own thoughts and actions". Personal agency is driven by the belief individuals have in themselves to exercise control over their own functioning.

Power, Capability: defined as the power or ability to do something, which we might think of in terms of an individual's awareness, knowledge, beliefs, mindsets and skills.

Power, Capacity: defined as the amount something can contain or produce, and for our purposes, we will think of this as competence.

Power Broker: affects the distribution, impact and influence of the collected power and value generated by the organisation.

Power generation: how people are empowered, how things get done and how information flows.

Power generators: The generation of power and value requires a source, capabilities, capacity and a receiver to amplify, conduct and distribute the power.

Power plant: The operations and processes of an organisation make up what we conceptualise as the mesh and we can think of as the power plant. The power plant provides capacity for information to flow through and generate value, ideally with minimal resistance.

Power source: contributors or clusters of contributors, such as the leadership team, are a source of empowerment to the surrounding mesh.

PRIMED: The acronym for the phases of a method that can be used to aid the continual process of organisational regeneration: Prepare; Run; Integrate; Manoeuvre; Evaluate; and Discover.

Psychological safety: a phrase coined by Amy Edmondson (see bibliography for reference) to describe a team environment where individuals feel safe to explore ideas, fail and iterate without fear of negative consequences.

RBBL: a practice for removing bias, barriers and limitations to gain awareness and expand thinking; to identify trapped and untapped value.

Remote work: where individuals employed by an organisation do not connect each day in a building but from geographically dispersed locations.

Self-awareness: describes an individual's understanding of themselves and their awareness about how they individually impact and respond to developments.

Self-efficacy: regulates human functioning and impacts cognitive, motivational, emotional, and choice processes.

Service Mesh: have advanced to solve security and visibility challenges presented by distributed technology, to connect them in a trusted way.

Smart contracts: enable granular, discrete contracts to be automatically executed, controlled or verified.

Tenets: set out the core values of the organisational culture and structure. Connection, Visibility and Trust are the Mesh tenets.

Tokenization: describes how assets (tokens) can be represented on a blockchain.

TUV: trapped & untapped value. Value that is available to an organisation but is not being used.

Trapped value: is any limitation or impediment that is creating an inability to realise a goal.

Untapped value: is overlooked, unseen or undervalued opportunities, connections and resources.

User-controlled data: is enabled by Web3, such as through user control of assets (tokens) listed on blockchains that might previously have been managed by an intermediary.

Value generation: can be thought of as the value that is generated by the contributions of individuals, teams and technologies.

Web3: the next stage of the world wide web; moves us on from the static web of limited connections and hyperlinks of Web1, past the dynamic web of ubiquitous creating, sharing and communication of Web2, to a decentralised, user-controlled web of Web3 including decentralisation, cryptocurrencies, tokenization, user-controlled data and smart contracts.

Bibliography

All the URLs listed in this bibliography were retrieved on 30 September 2022

101 Blockchains. (2022) The Ultimate Web3 Cheat Sheet. 101 Blockchains. https://101blockchains.com/web3-cheat-sheet

Agovino, T. (2019) To Have and to Hold. SHRM. URL: https://www.shrm.org/hr-today/news/all-things-work/pages/to-have-and-to-hold.aspx

Ashmore, D. (2022) A brief history of Web3.0. Forbes. URL: https://www.forbes.com/advisor/investing/cryptocurrency/what-is-web-3-0

Bandura, A. (1982) Self-efficacy mechanism in human agency. American psychologist, 37(2), 122

Bandura, A. (2001) Social Cognitive Theory and Clinical Psychology. International Encyclopedia of Social & Behavioral Sciences. 2001, p. 14250-14254. Pergamon. URL: https://doi.org/10.1016/B0-08-043076-7/01340-1

Bargh, J.A. & Morsella, E. (2008) The Unconscious Mind. Perspect Psychol Sci. 2008 Jan;3(1):73-9. National Library of Medicine

Berners-Lee, T. (1999) Weaving the Web: The Original Design and Ultimate Destiny of the World Wide Web by Its Inventor. HarperOne

Bitcoin. URL: https://bitcoin.org/en

Blanding, M. (2022) Want hybrid work to succeed? Trust, don't track employees. Harvard Business School

Calcote, L. et al (2023) Service Mesh Patterns. O'Reilly Media, Inc. URL: https://www.oreilly.com/library/view/service-mesh-patterns/9781492086444

Casilli, C. (2013) Badge pathways: part 0, the prequel. Persona Blog

Creative Commons. URL: https://creativecommons.org/about

Deci, E. & Ryan, R. (2000) Intrinsic and Extrinsic Motivations: Classic Definitions and New Directions. Contemporary Educational Psychology 25,54–67 (2000)

Deci, E. & Ryan, R. (2010) Intrinsic Motivation. The Corsini Encyclopedia of Psychology

Dehghani, Z. (2022) Data Mesh. O'Reilly Media, Inc.

De Meuse, K. (2017) Learning agility: Its evolution as a psychological construct and its empirical relationship to leader success. Consulting Psychology Journal: Practice and Research

Donne, J. (1624) MEDITATION XVII. Devotions upon Emergent Occasions

Duhigg, C. (2016) What Google Learned From Its Quest to Build the Perfect Team. The New York Times

Dweck, C. (2007) Mindset: The New Psychology of Success. Ballantine Books

Edmondson, A. (1999) Psychological Safety and Learning Behavior in Work Teams. Sage Publications

Ethereum. URL: https://ethereum.org/en

Farrer, L. (2020) 5 Proven Benefits Of Remote Work For Companies. Forbes. URL: https://www.forbes.com/sites/laurelfarrer/2020/02/12/top-5-benefits-of-remote-work-for-companies

Flynn, J. (1998) Taylor to TQM: 100 years of production management. IIE Solutions, October 1998, 22+. Gale Academic. URL: https://link.gale.com/apps/doc/A21221924/AONE?u=anon~1e54ec68&sid=googleScholar&xid=79deca83

Freeman, K. (2004) African Americans and College Choice. The Influence of Family and School. SUNY Press

Gigauri, I. (2021) New Economic Concepts Shaping Business Models In Post-Pandemic Era. International Journal of Innovative Technologies in Economy, (1(33). URL: https://doi.org/10.31435/rsglobal_ijite/30032021/7393

Gloat. (2021) Great Resignation Research Report. Gloat

Hamilton, G. (2016) Discussion Paper on Open Badges in Territories. Open Badge Network, Erasmus+. URL: www.openbadgenetwork.com/outputs/in-territories

Hamilton, G. & Blair, J. (2005) Online Collaborative Learning in Social Work Education (pdf). Ardcairn Publications

Hamilton, G. & Kelchner, J. (2021) Insights Report: At the Interchange of Open Culture & Navigating Futures (pdf). Interchange. URL: https://publications.interchange.world/wp-content/uploads/Insights-Summary-CY21-Open.pdf

Harman, P.H. (2002) The Scientific Letters and Papers of James Clerk Maxwell. Vol. III (1874-1879) Cambridge University Press

IBM. (2019) Do digital badges really provide value to businesses?. IBM.com. URL: https://www.ibm.com/blogs/ibm-training/do-digital-badges-really-provide-value-to-businesses

Innovate+Educate (2019) Shift Happens 2. Innovate+Educate. URL: https://issuu.com/innovate-educate/docs/shfithappens2

Khoury, G. & Crabtree, S. (2019) Are businesses worldwide suffering from a trust crisis? Gallup. URL: https://www.gallup.com/workplace/246194/businesses-worldwide-suffering-trust-crisis.aspx

Littlejohn, A. & Hood, N. (2017) How educators build knowledge and expand their practice: The case of open education resources. Br J Educ Technol, 48: 499-510. URL: https://doi.org/10.1111/bjet.12438

Malik, R., Visvizi, A. & Skrzek-Lubasińska, M. (2021) The Gig Economy: Current Issues, the Debate, and the New Avenues of Research. Sustainability 13, no. 9: 5023. MDPI. URL: https://doi.org/10.3390/su13095023

Markus, H & Nurius, P. (1986) Possible Selves. American Psychologist 41(9):954-969

Maslow, A.H. (1954) Motivation and personality. Harpers

Maxwell, J.C. (1865) A dynamical theory of the electromagnetic field. Philosophical Transactions of the Royal Society of London. 155: 459–512. URL: doi:10.1098/rstl.1865.0008

Mayes, T. (October 10th 1997) Dialogue with a Dumb Terminal. The Times Education Supplement

Mentour Pilot. URL: https://mentourpilot.com

Muir, J. (1911) My First Summer in the Sierra. Houghton Mifflin Company

Nicol, D. (2021) The power of internal feedback: exploiting natural comparison processes. Assessment and Evaluation in Higher Education, 46(5), pp. 756-778. URL: doi:10.1080/02602938.2020.1823314

Nicol, D. & Draper, S. (2009) A blueprint for transformational organisational change in higher education: reap as a case study. The Higher Education Academy

Open Badges. URL: https://openbadges.org

Painter, A., & Shafique, A. (2017) Cities of Learning in the UK Prospectus. RSA. URL: https://www.thersa.org/reports/cities-of-learning-prospectus

Parker, S. K. et al (2020) Remote Managers are Having Trust Issues. Harvard Business Review. URL: https://hbr.org/2020/07/remote-managers-are-having-trust-issues

Parker, S.K. & Menasce-Horowitz, J. (2022) Majority of workers who quit a job in 2021 cite low pay, no opportunities for advancement, feeling disrespected. Pew Research URL: https://www.pewresearch.org/fact-tank/2022/03/09/majority-of-workers-who-quit-a-job-in-2021-cite-low-pay-no-opportunities-for-advancement-feeling-disrespected

Pennington, H. (2019) Open source has a working-for-free problem. Tidelift. URL: https://blog.tidelift.com/open-source-has-a-working-for-free-problem

Peterson, C. (2018) How I 'coined' the term open source software. Opensource.com URL:

https://opensource.com/article/18/2/coining-term-open-source-software

Piaget, J. (1936) Origins of intelligence in the child. London: Routledge & Kegan Paul

PWC. (2022) Global Consumer Insights Pulse Survey June 2022. PWC URL: https://www.pwc.com/gx/en/industries/consumer-markets/consumer-insights-survey.html

Rowe, A. J. & Boulgarides, J. D. (1992) Managerial Decision Making. New York: Macmillan Publishing Company

RSA. (2015) The new digital learning age report. RSA.org. URL: https://www.thersa.org/reports/the-new-digital-learning-age

Sarkar, T.K., Salazar-Palma, M., & Sengupta, D. (2010) JAMES CLERK MAXWELL: The Founder of Electrical Engineering. Syracuse University

Savitz-Romer, M & Bouffard, M. (2012) Ready, Willing and Able. A Developmental Approach to College Access and Success. Harvard Education Press

Sidhpurwala, H. (2022) The art and science of secure open source software development. Red Hat

Siemens, G. (2004) Connectivism: A Learning Theory for the Digital Age. elearnspace

Simard, S. (2021) Finding the Mother Tree: Discovering the Wisdom of the Forest. Allen Lane

Sims, A. (2019) Blockchain and Decentralised Autonomous Organisations (DAOs): The Evolution of Companies? 28 New

Zealand Universities Law Review 423-458, URL: http://dx.doi.org/10.2139/ssrn.3524674

Taylor, F. (1911) The Principles of Scientific Management. Harper & Brothers

Testbook. (2022) Web 3-0. Testbook.com. URL: https://testbook.com/question-answer/with-reference-to-web-30-consider-the-fol--629dcb0ee276071a9078d530

The Mozilla Foundation et al. (2012) Open Badges for Lifelong Learning. Mozilla Foundation, URL: https://wiki.mozilla.org/images/5/59/OpenBadges-Working-Paper_012312.pdf

The Open Organization Ambassadors. (2017) The Open Organization Definition. The Open Organization. URL: https://theopenorganization.org/definition/open-organization-definition

Visier. (2022) Burnout Epidemic Report. Visier

Von Bernhardi, R. et al. (2017) What Is Neural Plasticity?. In: von Bernhardi, R., Eugenín, J., Muller, K. (eds) The Plastic Brain. Advances in Experimental Medicine and Biology, vol 1015. Springer, Cham

Vygotsky, L.S. (1978) Mind in society: the development of higher psychological processes. London: Harvard University Press

Westrum R. (2004) A typology of organisational cultures. Qual Saf Health Care. Suppl 2:ii22-7

Whitehurst, J. (2015) The Open Organization: Igniting Passion and Performance. Harvard Business Review Press

Whitman, W. (1855) Song of Myself, 51. Leaves of Grass. Walt Whitman

Wiles, J. (2022) Employees Seek Personal Value and Purpose at Work. Gartner. URL: https://www.gartner.com/en/articles/employees-seek-personal-value-and-purpose-at-work-be-prepared-to-deliver

Wiley, D. (2007) The MOOC Guide. The Wiley Wiki. URL: https://sites.google.com/site/themoocguide/cck08---mooc-basics

Wood, G. (2022) Polkadot's Gavin Wood on Building a Layer 0 to Underpin the Entire Blockchain-Based Economy. The Defiant Podcast, YouTube

About the Authors

Mesh represents over two decades of failures and successes by authors Gráinne Hamilton and Jen Kelchner, who have drawn on insights generated through their work to develop the Mesh organisational design.

They both thrive at frontiers and when pioneering new concepts to create better systems. They can be found creating open technology concepts, leading open communities, creating human-centric designs, helping leaders to improve performance, and organisations to digitally transform.

They have advised and partnered with technology giants, governments, Fortune 100 companies, universities, political unions, NGOs, global knowledge communities and cities, including the European Commission, Red Hat, Microsoft, Greenpeace, Deloitte, the Open Organization, Cities of Learning UK, the Bill & Melinda Gates Foundation, and the Mozilla Foundation. As founders of Interchange, they use Mesh when partnering with leaders and organisations to help them generate organisational success.

Gráinne Hamilton has contributed to innovations that have revolutionised how we learn, work and connect, from early work on open education and online learning with the University of Edinburgh, to concept architecting the award-winning Cities of Learning UK with the RSA, Open Badge Pathways with Mozilla, and Mesh. As an author of the Open Badge Standard she has influenced a global paradigm shift in how organisations think about learning and skills, from education institutions, to governments, to global Top 5 companies. She spent ten years helping universities digitally transform and enjoys partnering with leaders to shape conversations, design human-centric approaches and future-prime organisations.

Jen Kelchner is an engaging thought leader, ardent about revealing hidden work, removing limitations, human behaviours and pioneering the future. She has over 25 years of experience advising teams and senior leadership on performance improvement, architecting future pathways, releasing trapped and untapped value, and developing environments for high performing teams.

During her career at Deloitte and beyond, she has focused on workflow architecture, PMO leadership, M&A integration projects, operational cost opportunity, implementation strategies, concept models, executive coaching and team transformation.

She has created assessments and practices on open behaviours, removing limitations and on contribution tendencies which includes defining the human-centric components of Mesh; and, co-created the Open characteristics, Open Organization books and resources as well as assisting in architecting the global knowledge community, the Open Organization.

CPSIA information can be obtained
at www.ICGtesting.com
Printed in the USA
BVHW030845281122
652926BV00012B/169